CONTENTS

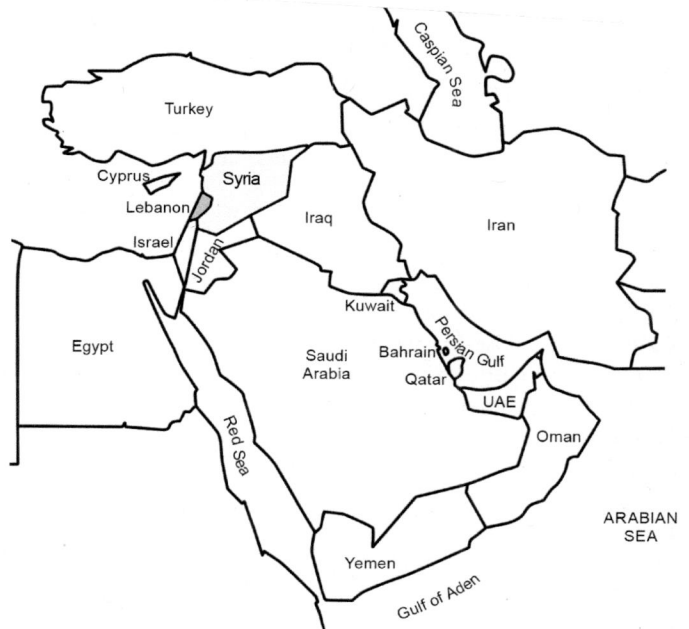

NOTE

In order to simplify the use of this book, all names, locations and geographic designations are as provided in *The Times World Atlas*, or other traditionally accepted major sources of reference, as of the time of the described events. Similarly, Arabic names are Romanised and transcripted rather than transliterated. For example: the definite article al- before words starting with 'sun letters' is given as pronounced instead of simply as al- (which is the usual practice for non-Arabic speakers in most English-language literature and media). Ranges and measurements cited in this book are provided in both metric and imperial measurements.

Helion & Company Limited

Unit 8 Amherst Business Centre, Budbrooke Road, Warwick CV34 5WE, England

Tel. 01926 499 619

Email: info@helion.co.uk   Website: www.helion.co.uk   Twitter: @helionbooks   Visit our blog http://blog.helion.co.uk/

Published by Helion & Company 2021

Designed and typeset by Farr out Publications, Wokingham, Berkshire

Cover designed by Paul Hewitt, Battlefield Design (www.battlefield-design.co.uk)

Text © Tom Cooper and Efim Sandler 2021

Photographs © as individually credited

Colour profiles © David Bocquelet & Tom Cooper 2021

Maps © Tom Cooper 2021

ISBN 978-1-914377-15-0

British Library Cataloguing-in-Publication Data.

A catalogue record for this book is available from the British Library.

For details of other military history titles published by Helion & Company Limited contact the above address, or visit our website: http://www.helion.co.uk. We always welcome receiving book proposals from prospective authors.

ABBREVIATIONS

AB	air base
ADF	Arab Deterrent Force
AFID	Air Force Intelligence Directorate (Syria)
ALA	*Armée du Liban Arabe* (also LAA)
ALF	Arab Liberation Front (Palestinians)
AMAL	Lebanese Resistance Regiments
AMAN	*Agaf HaModi'in* (Israeli military intelligence service)
ANO	Abu Nidal Organisation
APC	Armoured Personnel Carrier
ASCC	Air Standardisation Coordinating Committee
ATGM	Anti-Tank Guided Missile
CIWS	close-in weapon system
CO	commanding officer
CODOG	combined diesel or gas (powerplant)
COMINT	communications intelligence
DFLP	Democratic Front for the Liberation of Palestine
ECM	electronic countermeasures
FAL	*Force Aérienne Libanaise* (Lebanese Air Force)
HOT	*Hautsubsonique Optiquement Téléguidé Tiré d'un Tube* (High-subsonic, Optical, Remote-Guided, Tube-Launched) – French-built ATGM
HQ	Headquarters
IADS	integrated air defence system
IAI	Israeli Aircraft Industries
IDF	Israeli Defence Force
IDF/AF	Israeli Defence Force/Air Force
IED	improvised explosive device
IMI	Israeli Military Industries
INS	Israeli Navy Ship
LF	Lebanese Forces (Christian militia, Lebanon)
LNM	Lebanese National Movement (also *Mouvement National Libanais*, MNL)
LNM-JF	Lebanese National Movement – Joint Force
MANPAD	man-portable air defence system
MANTAK	Tank Directorate of the IDF
MASHA	Recovery and Maintenance Centre of the IDF
MBT	Main Battle Tank
MID	Military Intelligence Directorate/Division (Syria)
MiG	Mikoyan i Gurevich (the design bureau led by Artyom Ivanovich Mikoyan and Mikhail Iosifovich Gurevich, also known as OKB-155 or MMZ 'Zenit')
MRLS	multiple rocket launcher system
NATO	North Atlantic Treaty Organisation
NLP	National Liberal Party (Lebanon)
OKB	*Opytno-Konstrooktorskoye Byuro* (design bureau, USSR)
PFLP	Popular Front for the Liberation of Palestine (Palestinians)
PFLP-GC	Popular Front for the Liberation of Palestine – General Command (Palestinians)
PLA	Palestinian Liberation Army (Palestinians)
PLF	Palestinian Liberation Front (Palestinians)
PLO	Palestine Liberation Organisation (Palestinians)
PVO	*Protivovozdushnaya Oborona Strany* (Soviet Air Defence Force)
RAPAT	Tank Development Authority (Israel)
RPG	*Ruchnoy Protivotankoviy Granatomyot* (Hand-held anti-tank grenade launcher)
SAD	Defence Companies (Syria, predecessor to the Republican Guards Division)
SAM	surface-to-air missile
SIGINT	signals intelligence
SLA	South Lebanon Army (secular militia, Lebanon)
SPAAG	self-propelled anti-aircraft gun
SSNP	Syrian Socialist Nationalist Party (Lebanon)
Su	Sukhoi (the design bureau led by Pavel Ossipovich Sukhoi, also known as OKB-51)
SyAA	Syrian Arab Army
SyAADF	Syrian Arab Air Defence Force
SyAAF	Syrian Arab Air Force
UAV	unmanned/uninhabited aerial vehicle
UN	United Nations
UNIFIL	United Nations Interim Force in Lebanon
USAF	United States Air Force
USSR	Union of Soviet Socialist Republics (also 'Soviet Union')
ZLA	Zgharta Liberation Army (Maronite Christian militia, Lebanon)

INTRODUCTION AND ACKNOWLEDGEMENTS

Volume 1 of this series about the Lebanese Civil War served as an introduction to one of the most controversial and dramatic, and most tragic, civil wars of the late twentieth century, in which we provided a comprehensive insight into the millennia, and then centuries, decades and years that led to this conflict, and the forces involved, as a background to the recent tragedies. By comparison, Volume 2 covers only a relatively short period of about three years. The reason for this is that these three years not only demolished Lebanon but served as an overture for the even more fierce and more tragic conflicts in that country that were to follow – and then to last for decades. Furthermore, we have decided to document all of the operations of the Lebanese Christians against their opponents, and of Palestinian guerrilla operations against Israel in particular, and every single Israeli response – as thoroughly as necessary to understand the flow of events and patterns in behaviour of these parties. We have paid special attention to the many clashes between the Lebanese and Syrian forces, and Israeli and Syrian forces, because these had long-lasting consequences for the entire Middle East. Finally, we have paid attention to the role of Major Haddad and the so-called 'South Lebanon Army' (better known as the 'Free Lebanese Army' during 1978–81). In the course of preparing this review, we have taken care to clarify the political and military aims of all involved parties, as much as the operational patterns of their armed forces, their weaponry and tactics. The result is an in-depth and objective study, with an unusual flow of the narrative, but as complete at strategic, operational and tactical level as possible.

While our related research began at the time of the Israeli invasion of Lebanon in June 1982, it has really developed only in recent years, and thanks to the availability of the internet, which has enabled us to establish and maintain links with numerous participants and veterans of the Lebanese Civil War, and with other researchers and well-positioned contacts in the Middle

East and elsewhere. For their support in this project, we would like to thank to Albert Grandolini from France for providing much information and an extensive selection from his collection of photographs; Vatche Mitilian, Cesar Jachan and Samir Kassis from Lebanon for sharing from their extensive research on the Lebanese armed forces; Ali Tobchi from Iraq for sharing details from his own documentation and helping with translations from Arabic; Yosi Elmakis from Israel for help with precious recollections and photographs; Jamal Itani from Lebanon for help with crucial information and photographs; Nour Bardai from Egypt for helping in similar fashion; Jean-Marie Langeron from France and Tomislav Mesaric from Croatia for their immense help with detailed studies of US- and Soviet-made combat aircraft; Jeroen Nijmeijer for details on Soviet aircraft exports to the Middle East; Martin Smisek from Slovakia for sharing precious details on the Syrian armed forces; Pit Weinert from Germany for help with additional information and photographs; and Hicham Honeini from Lebanon for his help with translations of various publications in Arabic. Last but not least, Dr David Nicolle from Great Britain has been a source of encouragement and inspiration for this work over several decades, and has always been helpful with further information and photographs.

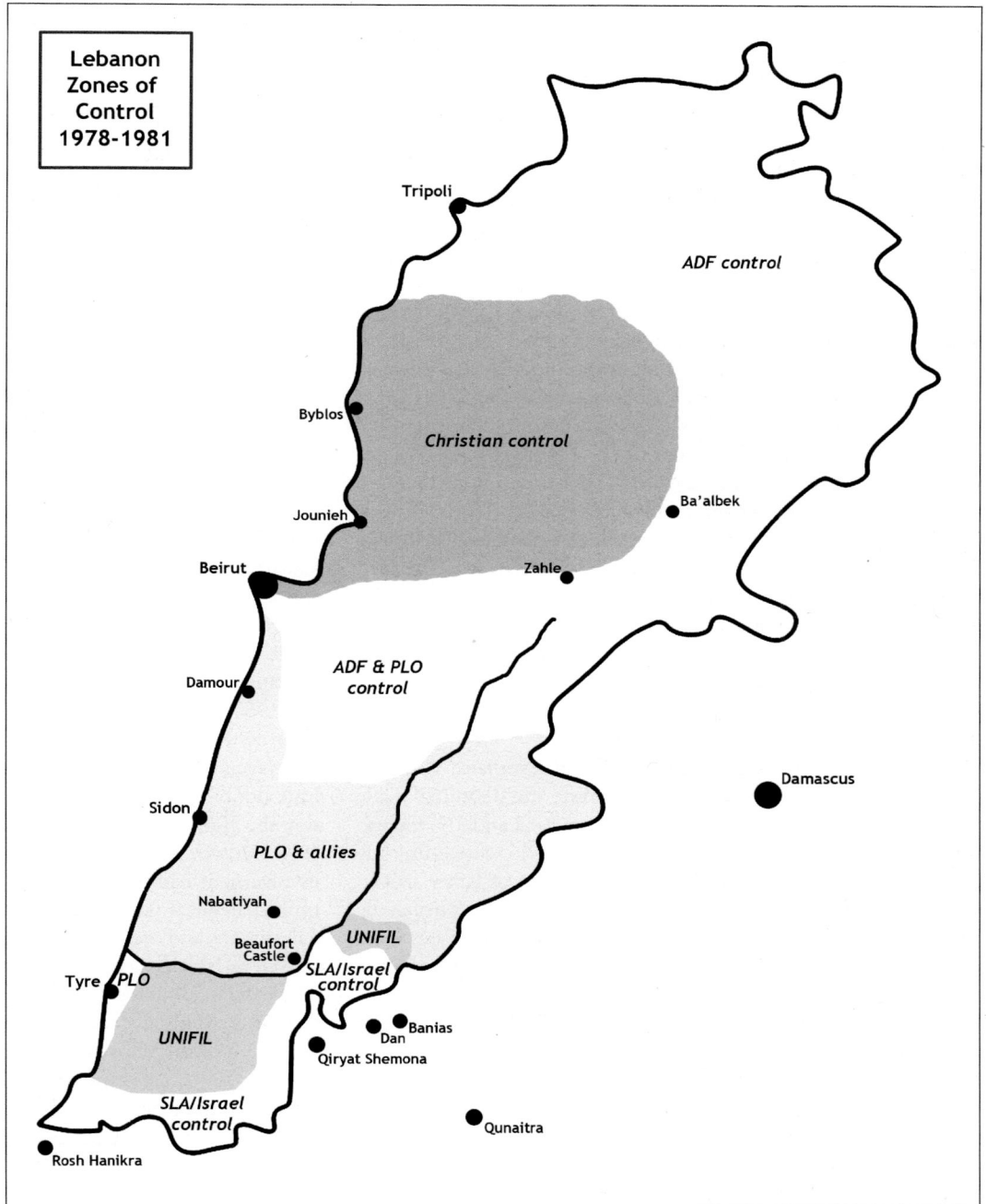

A map of Lebanon as of 1978, showing the approximate extent of enclaves controlled by local militias and foreign powers. (Map by Tom Cooper)

1

LEBANON OF 1978

If it took millennia of near-continuous conflict to set up the background and context for the war that erupted within the borders of Lebanon in 1975, events progressed at a much faster pace over the following years. Between 1975 and 1978, Lebanon ceased to exist as a sovereign country, disintegrating into dozens of enclaves controlled either by local and Palestinian militias or by foreign powers. For the easier understanding of the following events, the opening chapter of this volume provides a brief overview of the situation and the most important of the involved factions.

FAILED STATE

Created through unilateral action by the French Mandate authorities in 1920, Lebanon took less than half a century to emerge as a failed state. The principal reason for this was that the French imposed the Maronite Christian elites in a position of domination over a multi-sectarian country with a majority Muslim population. Of course, this is a massive oversimplification, because there existed numerous other differences between the country's 18 recognised religious groups and even more ethnic groups, and matters were not helped by the fact that no census was held after 1935. Assessments from the 1970s usually estimated the population of Lebanon at around 2–2.5 million, with Muslims making up between 55 and 61 percent of this number, and Christians between 29 and 35 percent. However, describing the Lebanese population as split into only these two religious groups would be a massive understatement: there were (and there remain) significant rifts between different sects of the major religions. Foremost among these splits is that between 23 and 29 percent of the Lebanese are Shi'a Muslims, and between 25 and 29 percent are Sunni Muslims. Traditionally, the majority of the Shi'a lived in southern Lebanon, West Beirut and the Beka'a Valley, while the Sunni Muslims lived in West Beirut, Tripoli and Sidon. While the Shi'a were generally kept away from positions of power, and could at most reach the position of the speaker of the parliament, Sunni notables traditionally held the state together – even if at most being eligible for the post of prime minister. Although only accounting for some 26–30 percent of the Lebanese population, Maronite Christians were granted the dominant positions in the economy and politics: indeed, the position of the president was (and remains) reserved for a Maronite Christian. However, Maronites were not the only Christian sect in the country: another 9 percent of the Lebanese were Eastern Orthodox Christians, while Melkite Catholics comprised up to 6 percent of the population and there were also Protestants, Roman Catholics as well as Armenian Apostolic and Armenian Catholic, Syriac Catholic and Syriac Orthodox, and Assyrian Christian communities, constituting another 5 percent. The majority of the Lebanese Christians populated Greater Beirut, northern Lebanon and the Mount Lebanon area. Last but not least, the Druze were usually assessed as constituting about 5 percent of the population, primarily in the rural, mountainous areas of Mount Lebanon and the Shouf Mountains.

Nominally, no Lebanese citizens were Palestinians, although they were very much present in the country, and definitely made the situation even more complex. Between 1947 and 1969, up to 400,000 Palestinian Muslims and Christians who were ethnically cleansed out of Palestine by the emerging state of Israel arrived in Lebanon. Even if many had since left (especially during the civil war), this number nearly doubled after numerous Palestinian militant organisations were evicted from Jordan during the so-called Black September of 1970. The majority of the Palestinians lived in 12 refugee camps: even if fewer than half of them were ever properly registered, their arrival, continuous presence, struggle for their own interests and rights, and continuous confrontations with Israel placed massive pressure upon the local economy, while they were not in the least welcomed by the government in Beirut or the powerful Christian minority. Keen to have Palestinians not only distanced from its own soil, but indeed to drive them ever further away from its borders, and plotting to re-establish Lebanon as a strong Christian-dominated state, Israel began openly destabilising the country – first through occasional raids that caused heavy damage to the local economy and infrastructure, and then though open assaults on the local population. The longer the Arab–Israeli conflict went on, the more Palestinians were welcomed by the Lebanese Muslims – particularly those opposing Christian dominance and Israeli involvement.

Last but not least, very few of the involved parties represented a monolithic political block: on the contrary, if all the above-mentioned differences of ethnic, religious and sectarian nature were not enough, it should be kept in mind that almost every single one of Lebanon's ethno-religious groups experienced its own differences over politics – within different communities (and especially those at least nominally 'Muslim') there were further rifts along ideological lines. The war that erupted in 1975 created additional refugees and resulted in the emergence of a large Lebanese diaspora: even if 'only' between 600,000 and 900,000 Lebanese left their homeland between 1976 and 1990, nowadays there are more people of Lebanese origin living abroad than in their home country. Their influence upon developments in the Lebanese Civil War remains almost as under-studied as the influence of most of the foreign powers that became involved.

WAR, IDEOLOGY – AND PROFITEERING

Unsurprisingly considering the above-mentioned conditions, and as described in Volume 1 of this work, the authority of the central government in Beirut began degenerating as early as the 1950s. Despite several major agreements at home and countless guarantees from abroad, the government disintegrated in the late 1960s and early 1970s, resulting in different parties creating their own para-states with their own administrations – and their own security forces, colloquially known as militias. There is little doubt that the spark that ultimately set the country on fire was the fighting between Maronite and Palestinian militants in 1975. However, an inter-ethnic war with Israeli and Palestinian involvement had been going on for years before this. By 1978, a multi-party war was pitting not only Maronite Christians against Palestinians and their allies, but also Christians against Christians, as well as Israelis against Palestinians and other Lebanese parties. The principal interests of all the parties involved could not have been more mutually exclusive, as the following illustrates:

- Generally, Christians insisted on retaining the position of dominance granted to them by the French. Blaming Israel for their misery, they entered into cooperation with Syria.

A memory from better times: a mixed formation led by seven Mirages, and including six Hunters, in one of the rare military parades in Beirut in 1971. (Albert Grandolini Collection)

A T-62 of the Syrian Army in a still from a video taken in Sidon in 1976. (Reuters)

- All the time perfectly aware of its economic and military superiority, Israel sought to drive the Palestinians – and their local allies – out of Lebanon, or at least to prevent them from bringing most of the country under their control. Furthermore, Israel sought to prevent the establishment of what it saw as a 'puppet Syrian regime', and to create an alliance with united Lebanese Christian forces.
- Palestinians sought to use Lebanon as a base for running a guerrilla war against Israel, and when such efforts were spoiled, gradually began creating a para-state within the country.
- Keen to subject the Palestinians in Lebanon to their control, and to prevent Israel from gaining a foothold in the country, thus outflanking their main front line on the Golan Heights, and to present themselves as the bulwark of the anti-Zionist struggle in the Arab world, the Syrians originally allied with the Christians and fought the Palestine Liberation Organisation (PLO).
- Multiple Lebanese left-wing and Muslim factions opposed not only the idea of a Christian-dominated Lebanon, but any kind of Israeli and/or Western influence and fought alongside the Palestinians against the Christians and the Israelis, while – via the PLO – securing much of their weaponry from the USSR and its allies.

If this was not enough, in what was certainly the biggest irony of this war, nearly all of the involved parties fought not only for the above-mentioned reasons, but also because the continuous armed conflict was stuffing the pockets of their leaders with cash. Myths about the 'existential threat' of the PLO's presence in Lebanon, and the 'prevention of Soviet penetration of the Middle East', safeguarded the continuous economic and military aid for Israel from the USA. Meanwhile, 'fighting against left-wing terror' – whether that of the Palestinians, local left-wing factions or 'Soviet puppets in Syria' – secured continuous economic and military aid for Christian factions from right-wing circles in Western Europe. Furthermore, the 'anti-Zionist' and 'anti-imperialist' struggle of the Palestinians and of local left-wing factions, secured them the support of both oil-wealthy Arab and conservative Arab governments, and the preparedness of the government of the Union of Soviet Socialist Republics (USSR/Soviet Union) and its allies in Eastern Europe to help. On top of all this, not only did every single faction involved in the Lebanese Civil War

receive one or another form of support from abroad, but by 1978 most of them had become involved in activities directly related to organised crime – including hashish production and smuggling of narcotics, and the trafficking of arms, supplies and stolen goods. As so often both before and after, all the leaders remained insistent in claiming to be the only legitimate authority with the 'good' and 'right' intentions and purposes – irrespective of whether they were seriously defending their communities or actually fighting for own economic and political interests.

MILITIA QUAGMIRE[1]

At the peak of the civil war, in late 1976, President Suleiman Frangieh of Lebanon invited the Syrian and other Arab armed forces into his country, thus prompting the creation of the Arab Deterrent Force (ADF). At the time, Frangieh did so with the full support of nearly all the Lebanese Christians, who thought that Syria would be able to force a ceasefire with the Palestinians and protect the Christians. Furthermore, understanding that the civil war was not only a showdown between the Maronites and Christians, Frangieh also attempted to end the conflict through consensus, by reducing the power of the Maronites and establishing parity between Christians and Muslims in the Lebanese Parliament. Initially supported by the majority of influential politicians and religious leaders, this initiative ultimately failed. Indeed, the idea of peace through consensus remained impossible even once the National Assembly elected Youssef Sarkis as the new president on 8 May 1976. Although – or precisely because – Sarkis was another Syrian ally, his attempts to forge a lasting accommodation between Christian and Muslim factions failed due to opposition from the conservatives, but especially because the left-wing forces – reinforced through their cooperation with the PLO – felt emboldened to the degree that they insisted it was too late to settle for perfunctory changes in the political landscape.

Meanwhile, ignoring the fact that immense Soviet pressure had forced the government in Damascus to stop fighting the PLO, and that his attempts to fight the Palestinians exposed President Hafez al-Assad to both a growing insurgency at home and unrest within his armed forces, the leaders of the right-wing Lebanese Christian parties concluded that Syria could not impose a solution acceptable to them, but was solely pursuing its own interests. Disappointed, they intensified their contacts with Israel instead. Originally, this idea alone was anathema to them: although Christians, the Maronites were (and still are) Arabs, and they blamed Israel for their problems with Palestinians (up to 10 percent of whom were Christians too). However, by 1978, occasional meetings and small-scale deliveries of arms and ammunition – always conducted under conditions of great secrecy – gradually turned into an almost-permanent presence of advisors in the form of Israeli intelligence officers. Over the following two years, anathema made way for dogma about the Maronites and the Jews sharing a common fate,

One of the Israeli-supplied M50 Shermans of the Christian militias, seen in 1979. All Israeli-supplied tanks and armoured personnel carriers were painted in grey, while some had additional disruptive camouflage patterns in dark grey on top of that. (Photo by Yosi Elmakis)

The crew of a Phalangist M113 climbing onto their vehicle. (Efim Sandler Collection)

a miscellany of M38A1 and M151 jeeps, Land Rovers and other pick-ups that usually mounted either a machine gun or a recoilless rifle, and a small armoured 'corps' operating a handful each of AMX-13s, M41s, M42s, M113s and Panhard M3 VTT APCs. Starting in 1979, the Tigers began receiving quantities of US-made M50 Sherman medium tanks, M16 assault rifles and M72 light anti-tank weapons from Israel.

The Chamouns' decision to ally with Israel was followed by Pierre Gemayel, leader of the Lebanese Christian Kataeb Party and in control of the most powerful of the Maronite Christian militias of Lebanon in 1978, the Kataeb Regulatory Forces (KFR, colloquially the 'Kataeb' or 'Phalange'). Headquartered in Bikfaya – the feudal seat of the Gemayel family – thanks to support from the Lebanese Army, Egypt, Jordan and right-wingers in Belgium, France and Spain, the KFR included about 2,000 full-time regulars and up to 3,000 reservists. They were armed with a similar miscellany of AMX-13s and M41s, M42s and AML-90s as the Tigers, but also operated US-made armoured cars, such as the Cadillac Cage V-100 Commando and T17E Staghound. Crucial to Gemayel's decision to side with Israel was his son, Bashir, who – back in 1976 – was the only Maronite leader to oppose an alliance with Syria, and who became highly popular among his combatants both for propagating the idea of a 'new Lebanon' – free of factionalism, feudalism and corruption – and for his leadership qualities.

and it only being to their mutual benefit if they fought together against the PLO and Syria.

Two strongmen in the Maronite community led this process. Camille Chamoun, a former President of Lebanon and leader of the National Liberal Party (NLP), was the first to burn bridges with the Arab world and to turn to Israel. Chamoun's son, Dany, led the 3,500–4,000-strong Ahrar militia (colloquially 'Tigers'), of which about 500 were full-time, regular fighters (the others being reservists), and who included both deserters from the army and civilians. Originally supported by the USA, Egypt, Iran and Jordan, the Ahrar operated mainly in East Beirut, Jbeil and Tripoli, but had some presence in the Beka'a Valley too. It was armed with

Both the Tigers and the Phalange were severely weakened during the fighting of 1975–76, when they lost well over 1,000 combatants killed. However, with support from Israel (which reached a value of about US$150 million by 1981), Bashir Gemayel reorganised the Phalange, appointed his young loyalists in key positions and, in late 1977, entered a loose alliance with the Tigers and a few minor Christian militias, including the Tanzim and the Guardians of the Cedars. By early 1978, they were about 5,000 strong when fully mobilised, and comprised armour, artillery and commando units, their own naval service and a very

A worn out BTR-152 armoured personnel carrier of the Guardians of the Cedars in south Lebanon in 1978. (The National Library of Israel)

advanced intelligence branch. While most of their armament was still drawn from stocks of the Lebanese armed forces, by 1978–79 they were openly advised and supported by Israel.

However, it was precisely Gemayel's and Chamoun's cooperation with Israel that prevented the third major Maronite militia – the Zgharta Liberation Army (ZLA, colloquially 'Marada') – from joining the new alliance. The ZLA – controlled by Suleiman Frangieh and commanded by his son, Tony – comprised about 3,500 fighters (some 800 were full-time combatants and 1,500 irregulars), organised into three brigades (the strongest was the Marada Brigade, commanded by Tony Frangieh), but remained in alliance with the Syrians.

The fourth predominantly Christian militia of Lebanon in this period was – at least nominally – secular by nature. By 1978, it crystallised in the form of the Free Lebanon Army (from 1983 the South Lebanon Army, SLA – a designation in use until its demise and used in this project for the purpose of easier understanding). Created in cooperation between the Lebanese government, Camille Chamoun and Israel with the aim of reforming and regrouping the remnants of Lebanese Army units and various militias opposed to the PLO and the Syrians, and still present in the south of the country, the SLA was led by Major Sa'ad Haddad of the Lebanese Army. It worked in full coordination with the Israeli Defence Forces (IDF), even if – at least nominally – being subjected to the Israel-based 'Government of Free Lebanon'. Thanks to advice and donations of surplus arms from IDF stocks, the SLA was a well-trained force organised into two regions (western and eastern), each of which had one infantry brigade consisting of three battalion-sized infantry regiments, supported by a total of about 50 Israeli-upgraded M50 Shermans and Soviet- and Czechoslovak-made T-54/55 main battle tanks (MBTs), of which the majority were significantly upgraded in Israel. Furthermore, the SLA operated a handful of French-made AMX-13 light tanks and M3 halftracks of US design and manufacture, donated by Israel. It was mainly its artillery – including a mix of British-made 25-pdrs, a few French-made BF-50s, Soviet-made M-46 field guns and a wide array of light anti-aircraft pieces – that made this force so powerful.

The small and disparately organised Lebanese Armed Forces fell apart during 1975 and 1976, but thanks to the presence of the ADF, serious efforts were already underway for their reconstruction. Therefore, while much of their personal and heavy equipment – including old Charioteer and Sherman medium tanks, AMX-13 and M41 Walker Bulldog light tanks, M42 self-propelled anti-aircraft guns (SPAAGs), armoured personnel carriers (APCs), armoured cars and artillery – ended up in the hands of various (particularly Christian) militias, numerous units were reorganised and undergoing renewed training. That said, the sole branch that remained intact – the Lebanese Air Force (*Force Aérienne Libanaise*, FAL) – was effectively grounded. Although still in control of its aircraft (including seven Hawker Hunter F.Mk 70 fighter-bombers, two Hunter T.Mk 66 two-seat conversion trainers, 10 Dassault Mirage IIIEL interceptors, two Mirage IIIBL conversion trainers and a miscellany of light and training aircraft and helicopters) and its most important facility – the Ryak Air Base (AB) – it hardly ever flew, and was never again to exercise effective control over its own airspace.

LEBANESE LEFTIST AND MUSLIM MILITANT GROUPS[2]

That the Lebanese Civil War was a far cry from the usually reported 'Maronites vs Palestinians' conflict becomes obvious once one considers that by 1978 it involved a large number of left-wing and Muslim militias, the majority of which fought as allies of the PLO. The mass of such groups operated within the aegis of the Lebanese National Movement (LNM, but at the time better known under its French title, *Mouvement National Libanais*, MNL). Originally led by Kamal Jumblatt – traditional leader of the Druze community and a former prime minister of Lebanon – the MNL was an alliance of leftist, pan-Arabist and Syrian nationalist parties and movements. Its militia was originally named the Common Forces, but became best known as the Joint Forces (LNM-JF). Following the Damascus-staged dissolution of the Arab Liberation Army (ALA), as of 1978, the LNM-JF mostly consisted of the People's Liberation Army and the Popular Guard (the latter being the militia of the Syrian Socialist National Party, SSNP), the militias of the pro-Iraqi wing and the pro-Syria wing of the Ba'ath Party and the pan-Arabist militia. Altogether, the LNM-JF had about 18,000 active combatants, mostly poorly trained civilians, and included relatively few defectors from the Lebanese Army.

Perhaps the most interesting – and certainly the most often ignored – element of the LNM-JF alliance was the al-Mourabitoun ('The Sentinels'): the military wing of the Independent Nasserite Movement. Originally founded in 1957 in Beirut as opposition to the pro-Western policies of then-President Camille Chamoun, and actively involved in the Civil War of 1958, this party experienced a decline in the 1960s but re-emerged as a major political faction within the Sunni Muslim community of the mid-1970s. Its al-Mourabitoun militia was re-established in 1975 around a cadre of only some 120–150 fighters, but rapidly grew to between 3,000 and 5,000 men drawn from Muslim quarters of West Beirut, commanded by Ibrahim Kulaylat. Initially at least, it was allied with the PLO and opposed Syria, and thus was mostly

Combatants of the Amal during a house-to-house battle against the PLO in 1976. (Albert Grandolini Collection)

Members of the al-Mourabitoun monitoring a knocked out M3 halftrack of one of the Christian militias. (Albert Grandolini Collection)

itself to an exclusively Sunni force but did not lose its military capabilities. By 1981, it controlled most of West Beirut and was capable of running its own media services, including a radio and then a television station.

Another new appearance on the stage of the Lebanese Civil War in the late 1970s was the Harakat Amal ('The Movement of the Deprived'). Initially little more than 'another little militia' of the Lebanese Civil War, it was founded by Musa as-Sadr and the Greek Catholic Archbishop of Beirut in 1974, thus attracting support from many different persuasions. However, following the Israeli Operation Stone of Wisdom, which caused massive destruction and widespread suffering of civilians in southern Lebanon, the Amal began recruiting primarily from the underrepresented Shi'a population. By 1980 – by when it was led by Nabih Berri – it was the largest Shi'a party in the Lebanese parliament. Allied with Syria, the Amal was at odds with the Palestinians; not only reasonably well-equipped, it boasted a strength of up to 14,000 combatants.

PALESTINIAN FACTIONS[3]

Since relocating most of its combatants to Lebanon in 1970, the armed groups making up the Palestinian Liberation Organisation grew into the most potent fighting force in Lebanon – even if the organisation remained little more than a loose confederation of disparate militant factions. The PLO was led by Yasser Arafat and dominated by Fatah, the core ideology of which was of an ill-defined nationalist direction, actually centred on the idea of conducting a guerrilla war for the liberation of Palestine. The organisation was funded by nearly all of the oil-exporting countries in the Arab world, but predominantly Saudi Arabia, Iraq and Libya, and had the USSR as its primary source of arms. In 1970, the PLO's cadre was strongly bolstered by a large number of highly experienced defectors from the Jordanian Army. By 1978, it was freely recruiting from the huge Palestinian refugee camps of Lebanon, and its combatants were operating freely over most of the country between Beirut in the north and the Litani River in the south. However, even though having the concept of a regular army (*Jaysh Nizami*), the PLO was slow in realising this – for a variety of reasons. While military ranks were introduced and the first independent artillery units created

armed with weapons and equipment of Soviet origin provided by Libya and Egypt. During the fighting of 1975–76, it captured numerous armoured vehicles, including at least two Sherman Fireflies and several Charioteer medium tanks, some M42s and AML-90s and a handful of M113s and Panhard M3 VTT APCs. The al-Mourabitoun operated a significant artillery component too, including Soviet-made 57mm ZiS-2 and 76.2mm ZiS-3 guns, 122mm M1938 122mm howitzers, 130mm Type-59-1 field guns, at least five 122mm BM-11 and BM-21 MRLS systems and numerous ZU-23 automatic anti-aircraft cannons (the majority of which were mounted on Toyota Land Cruiser and similar pickup trucks – so-called 'technicals'). The al-Mourabitoun quickly earned themselves a reputation for being stubborn and determined fighters, highly effective in applying guerrilla tactics in urban areas. However, heavy casualties and atrocities against non-Muslims, followed by internal splits among its leadership, caused many defections. Always fiercely anti-Israel, in 1977–78 the movement came to terms with the Syrians and converted

A group of Palestinian militants in southern Lebanon in the late 1980s. (Photo by Francois Lochon)

A BM-14 multiple rocket launcher of the PLO in action during the early stages of the Lebanese Civil War. (Albert Grandolini Collection)

the Syrians or their Lebanese allies in conventional warfare. From 1975–77, and thanks to continuously growing funding and Soviet support, the organisation found it relatively easy to establish three conventional brigades:

• Castel Force, deployed in the Sidon–Tyre–Amun–Nabattiyyeh area
• Yarmouk Force, deployed in the Jezzine area
• Karama Force, deployed in the Arqub

Each of these units (their combined strength was around 8,500 men) had a company-worth of T-34/85 medium tanks and a battery of D-30 122mm howitzers, at least a few M-46 130mm guns, a platoon of BM-21 122mm multiple rocket launchers and a platoon each of BRDM-2 armoured scout cars and BTR-152 APCs. The balance of the PLO consisted of about 6,000–7,000 irregulars deployed with the LNM-JF in Beirut, about 4,000 (including Lebanese allies) in south Lebanon and 3,000 in Beka'a and Tripoli. They were controlled from two headquarters:
• Forward Command in Tyre, led by Azami Zarayer
• Main Command in Sidon, under Haj Ismail (who also served as the Castel Force commander)[4]

in 1973–74, no assets bigger than a company are known to have existed before the outbreak of the Lebanese Civil War. The conflict accelerated the further growth of different armed groups making up the PLO, and then by an order of magnitude, but most remained guerrilla-oriented by nature, and – at least early on – continued preparing for the fighting of such a war against Israel. However, during the Lebanese Civil War, the Palestinians found themselves fighting significantly different enemies on at least three fronts at the same time. One was the massively superior Israel, which enjoyed all the advantages in training, equipment, firepower and manoeuvre, experience and intelligence and fought in the form of raids by special forces and by conventional troops. Another was Syria, which fought with a mix of conventional troops reinforced by what it designated commandos and special forces. Finally, various different Lebanese militias usually fought conventionally, forcing the Palestinians to hold – and to fight along – extended stretches of static front lines. These circumstances forced the PLO into developing a very flexible military strategy: it had to face the Israelis with guerrilla warfare, with small and scattered units, but also had to concentrate men and equipment whenever fighting

Despite such growth and imposing military strength, the PLO not only suffered extensive losses during the Lebanese Civil War (about 1,000 regular combatants, or some 20 percent of its force), but also never stopped suffering from disunity in its political leadership and lack of experienced military commanders. Even Yasser Arafat – highly popular within the population of the Gaza Strip and the West Bank – was hotly disputed because, following years of armed struggle, he began propagating diplomacy in public and supported a proposal for a UN Security Council resolution calling for a two-state solution for Israel and Palestine, based on borders before the June 1967 Arab–Israeli War. The idea was not only vetoed by the USA and refused by Israeli right-wingers but opposed by the majority of other Palestinian leaders. In turn, the fact that Fatah dominated the PLO, and Arafat was in charge, caused him to create deep rifts with the organisation of his primary rival – the Popular Front for the Liberation of Palestine (PFLP). This movement fell apart into several splinter groups, including the Democratic Front for the Liberation of Palestine (DFLP) and the Palestinian Liberation Front (PLF). That said, dozens

Yasser Arafat, leader of Fatah, the strongest faction within the Palestinian Liberation Organisation – and the leader of the PLO. (Albert Grandolini Collection)

A Dutch YP-408 APC deployed with UNIFIL in Lebanon. (via Efim Sandler)

of other armed Palestinian factions also existed, most of which operated outside the aegis and influence of the PLO. Foremost among these was the as-Sa'iqa, controlled by Damascus and the Palestinian Liberation Army (PLA), operating as an element of the Syrian armed forces. In similar fashion, Baghdad exercised control over the group naming itself the Arab Liberation Front (ALF). Finally, groups such as the Abu Nidal Organisation (ANO) and the Popular Front for the Liberation of Palestine – General Command (PFLP-GC) included extremists who de-facto acted as freelances, sometimes under Syrian, other times under Iraqi or Libyan orders, in exchange for their support: they became notorious for numerous high-profile terrorist attacks, not all of which were directly related to Israel.

PEACEKEEPING FORCES: THE ADF AND UNIFIL[5]

The Arab Deterrent Force (ADF) was an international peacekeeping force created by the Arab League during the extraordinary summit in Riyadh of October 1976, in reaction to the escalation of the Lebanese Civil War. Deployed in Lebanon from November that year, it included about 25,000 troops of the Syrian

Arab Army (SyAA) and a mix of smaller units from Libya, Saudi Arabia, Sudan and the United Arab Emirates. The ADF's mandate was to deter the conflicting parties from once again resorting to violence, maintain the ceasefire, collect the various groups' heavy weapons and help the Lebanese government restore its authority. The headquarters of the ADF were in the town of Chtoura, in the Beka'a Valley and as of 1978 it was commanded by Major General Samy al-Khatib. The Syrian component consisted of the 35th and 41st Special Forces Brigades, 47th and 62nd Mechanised Infantry Brigades, 51st Independent Armoured Brigade and 67th Independent Brigade: a significant portion of the latter two units was encamped around the town of Zahle, in the upper Beka'a (predominantly populated by Greek Orthodox Christians), but most of the force was heavily present in West Beirut, Tripoli, Sidon and the Shouf Mountains. The ADF had next to no presence in East Beirut and absolutely none in southern Lebanon.

At least initially, the ADF's activity was reasonably effective. It managed to collect thousands of light arms and dozens of heavy guns, largely from the PLO, while also providing security for the

A T-54/55 of the Syrian contingent of the ADF in the Zahle area, near the Beirut–Damascus road (visible in the background), together with a miscellany of utility vehicles. Note the turret number 452 and the white stripes used for easier identification. (Albert Grandolini Collection)

A pair of YP-408 eight-wheeled armoured personnel carriers of the Dutch battalion of UNIFIL in 1980. (UN)

buying time to solidify the SLA's position. Meanwhile, the PLO, understanding that if the peacekeepers were allowed to carry out their mandate it would be deprived of territory and routes of approach to Israel, set out to re-establish its presence in the area. Indeed, to demonstrate its preparedness to fight, in May 1978 it ambushed a UNIFIL patrol, killing three and wounding 10 of its troops, and then began re-establishing minor bases within the nominally UN-controlled zone. The UN peacekeeping mission was thus literally cowed and compromised by both the Israelis and the Palestinians.[6]

people to the degree that the economy was reactivated and banks reopened. The ADF's biggest success took place on 21 July 1977, when its presence proved instrumental in convincing Palestinian factions to withdraw all their combatants 15km from the Israeli border. However, the Arab Deterrent Force never managed – nor was effectively authorised or deployed – to prevent continuous low-level clashes between the Christians and Palestinians, or the continuously intensifying turmoil further south in Lebanon. Moreover, it soon became involved in distributing arms and ammunition to pro-Syrian factions in Beirut, resulting in accusations that Syria was acting as an occupying power rather than a peacekeeping force.

Ironically, the ADF was not the only peacekeeping force deployed in Lebanon during 1978. Officially established on 19 March 1978 – in reaction to the Israeli Operation Stone of Wisdom (see Volume 1 of this work for details) – the United Nations Interim Force in Lebanon (UNIFIL) was a peacekeeping mission with the mandate to monitor and verify a complete and unconditional withdrawal of the IDF from the country and to help the Lebanese government restore its effective authority along its southern border with Israel. The first UNIFIL troops deployed in southern Lebanon on 23 March 1978, and consisted of troops redeployed from other UN peacekeeping operations in the Middle East. Eventually, the UN contingent included seven reinforced infantry battalions – about 4,000 troops – from Algeria, Fiji, Ghana, Ireland, The Netherlands and Senegal, with company-sized detachments from France, Norway and Sweden. The first UNIFIL commander was Major General Emmanuel S. Alexander Erskine, from Ghana, a professional officer trained in Great Britain at the Royal Military Academy at Sandhurst, the Staff College at Camberley and the Royal College of Defence Studies, and with experience from similar missions in Egypt and Israel between 1974 and 1978. UNIFIL's primary task was to supervise an immediate and unconditional Israeli withdrawal, and then make sure that southern Lebanon was not used for hostile actions of any kind, regardless by what party. However, instead of acting on orders from New York – and as demanded by the administration of President Jimmy Carter in Washington DC – Erskine and his aides did not react when the IDF violated the ceasefire that ended Operation Stone of Wisdom, and then began bargaining for its conquests north of the Litani River, in turn

Israelis and the Palestinians.[6]

2

THE HUNDRED DAYS' WAR

The fighting between 1975 and 1978 deeply scarred Lebanon. Most damage was caused by hundreds – if not thousands – of direct attacks on the civilian population, with massacres, (Israeli) air raids, artillery bombardments of densely populated areas (by all involved parties), raids, looting, rape and the forced displacement of hundreds of thousands of people. This murderous combination had created deep hatred on all sides, nearly a million refugees and sectarian-based, homogenous cantons, transforming the country's demographics forever. Unsurprisingly considering the involvement of so many disparate Lebanese factions and various foreign powers, and the ineffectiveness of the international community, the truces resulting from the deployment of the ADF and UNIFIL in 1977 all soon proved untenable – and for this nearly everybody involved was to blame. At least when it comes to the ADF, there is little doubt that there was one discipline in which it failed abysmally: it proved unable to prevent a string of small-scale massacres and assassinations of Christians in Beirut and the Shouf throughout 1977 and early 1978, which caused the death of several hundred people, with an additional 200,000 having to flee their homes. Eventually, it was precisely this factor that led to the collapse of the strategic alliance between the Lebanese Christians and the Syrians.

SECOND BATTLE OF FAIYADIYEH[1]

Aghast by what he saw as the failure of the ADF to act in defence of Christians, in early 1978, not only Chamoun and Gemayel, but even Frangieh began to openly call for a withdrawal of Syrian troops from Lebanon. Before long, their militias and Syrian troops became embroiled in a growing number of incidents at numerous checkpoints held by the latter. As tensions continued mounting, the situation escalated to the point where the Lebanese demanded the ADF remove the Syrian checkpoint from the entrance to the camp at Faiyadiyeh in the south-eastern outskirts of Beirut, near the road connecting the Lebanese capital to Damascus in Syria, only some 40km away. Inside the camp were about 1,500

Lebanese soldiers, primarily Christians, but also some Druze and Muslims, including 300 cadets of the Military Academy, 700–800 recruits undergoing elementary training, 200 military police and 49 officers.

Under pressure, the Syrians removed their checkpoint and announced that overall command of the garrison was now in the hands of Captain Samir al-Ashgar of the Lebanese Army. Instead, early on 7 February, the Syrians set up a new checkpoint at the nearby Rihaniya junction, close to the Syrian Embassy and directly in front of the Maghawir al-Aghar camp, which included the building of the Lebanese Ministry of Defence. Only hours later, a unit of the Lebanese Army returning from an exercise was stopped and its troops searched. As this was going on, a large crowd of civilians gathered around the scene: eventually, several of them attacked the Syrian troops, took away their arms and opened fire. The Syrians fired back and more than 20 people were killed in the ensuing firefight.

Alerted by this incident so close to the Syrian Embassy, Major General Khatib ordered Syrian troops of the ADF to the scene. His commanders hurriedly deployed a regiment of undertrained reservists, usually tasked only with guard duties. In the meantime, Captain Ashgar put the troops in the Faiyadiyeh camp on alert and deployed them for perimeter defence. He went as far as to position several teams operating Browning M2 machine guns in sandbagged positions on the second floor of houses across the street from the main entrance, from where they had clear lines of fire at the street below and the nearby road connecting Beirut with Damascus. Additional machine guns and teams armed with Soviet-made RPG-7 rocket-propelled grenades were positioned on top of the roofs of higher buildings, and sandbagged for better protection. Inside the base, Ashgar had all troops armed and deployed, and three D-30 122mm howitzers brought up to provide direct fire against any vehicles attempting to enter the camp or approach along the Beirut–Damascus highway. Moreover, he ordered the few available Staghound armoured cars into position between the buildings. Finally, Ashgar established a forward position about 150 metres outside the eastern side of the barracks. Initially, this included two AMX-13 light tanks – each equipped with a 105mm CN-105 gun in a FL-12 turret – and an infantry platoon positioned to the east of the Beirut–Damascus road. This outpost was eventually bolstered by six M42 Dusters and about 80 troops armed with machine guns and RPG-7s, in a position stretching to the high ground south of the barracks and Faiyadiyeh village. For all practical purposes, Ashgar had set up a deadly trap for the Syrians.

Unsuspecting, the latter approached Faiyadiyeh camp in a column of trucks around noon, only to run straight into crossfire from howitzers, machine guns and RPG-7s from multiple directions.

Dozens of Syrian troops were killed within seconds: whoever still could, scrambled for whatever cover was available, only to be pinned down well inside the killing zone. At the sight and sound of the scene in front of them, the following units refused to attack, prompting Khatib to rush additional reinforcements to Faiyadiyeh. Eventually, four infantry regiments, three battalions of commandos, a company of T-55 MBTs, a battery with four D-30 howitzers, two ZU-23 anti-aircraft guns and a platoon of jeeps mounting B-10 82mm recoilless rifles were deployed by the Syrian Arab Army in the combat zone. As soon as everything was ready, during the afternoon of 7 February, the Syrians attempted to attack with their T-55s, but their armour-piercing ammunition proved ineffective against the buildings of Faiyadiyeh camp, made of solid, 25cm-thick sandstone and reinforced concrete. Facing intensive fire from numerous RPG-7s and 105mm cannons of the two AMX-13s, the Syrians withdrew, after which their T-55s provided only fire support.

A new attempt – this time to reach the troops still pinned down in front of the entrance to the camp – was launched on the morning of 8 February, once again by T-55s. However, during the night, Ashgar had deployed one of his RPG-7 teams into a forward position and, operating from the second floor of a dominating building, they quickly knocked out one MBT with a direct hit to the turret. One of the Syrian jeeps mounting a B-10 recoilless rifle was then put out of action while trying to cover the crew of the destroyed tank. After this, the Syrians gave up and, on 9 February, Khatib ordered his troops to stop where they were, pending negotiations between President Sarkis and Abdul Halim Khaddam, the foreign minister of the Syrian Arab Republic. Sarkis and Khaddam agreed to set up a truce and then conduct an investigation into the causes of the fighting.

As often in this conflict, only half the agreement was carried out. The total death toll of the three-day-long 'Second Battle of Faiyadiyeh' was estimated at about 150 killed and 250 wounded, mostly SyAA troops. Unsurprisingly, Damascus remained insistent on a full investigation and courts-martial for all the Lebanese officers

Several Staghound armoured cars of the Lebanese Army were involved in the Second Battle of Faiyadiyeh from 7–9 February 1978. This example was captured by the Lebanese Arab Army and frequently deployed against its former owners. (Albert Grandolini Collection)

and other ranks who were responsible. On 23 February, during a meeting at the Ba'abda Palace in Beirut, Major General Khatib presented a list of 12 officers and non-commissioned officers to Lebanese Minister of Defence Fouad Boutros and Victor Khoury, Commander-in-Chief of the Lebanese Army. Initially at least, the Lebanese flatly turned down his demands for the responsible troops to be arrested and prosecuted. However, when Damascus increased pressure, Captain Ashgar, 1st Lieutenant Fares Ziadeh, Lieutenant Antoine Haddad and two soldiers were arrested the next day and subjected to a Special Security Court. Ironically, this inquiry issued no rulings regarding what they did. Nevertheless, Ashgar refused to accept prosecution for what he considered was performance of his duty. Feeling unfairly treated, he defected and established a new militia: the Revolutionary Command of the Lebanese Army. In a twist of fate, the Lebanese officer was eventually killed, on 1 November the same year, during a clash with the Lebanese Army.

OUT OF CONTROL[2]

The clash at Faiyadiyeh camp marked the start of an open confrontation between the reconstituted Lebanese Army, the Christian militias and the ADF in what was known as the Hundred Days' War. It began with Bashir Gemayel and Camille Chamoun instigating demonstrations against the presence of Syrian troops.

In Damascus, the government of Hafez al-Assad was publicly presenting Syria as the geopolitical heart of the Middle East (and as such a maker of peace and war), a country to which – historically – Lebanon, Jordan and what was left of the Arab Palestine belonged, and as the only active champion of Arab rights, standing alone in the way of a Zionist walkover. As such, Hafez could not tolerate anybody in Lebanon trying to sideline him. He went so far as to deliver an ultimatum: the Maronites were to lay down their arms and permit the deployment of ADF troops in East Beirut, or their strongholds there would be taken by force. Without waiting for the ultimatum to expire, he ordered Minister of Defence Mustafa Tlas and the Chief-of-Staff of the Syrian Arab Army, Lieutenant General Hikmat Chebabi, into action: thereafter, for most of 9 February 1978, helicopters of the Syrian Arab Air Force (SyAAF) airlifted commandos from several special forces regiments to Beirut.[3]

When Assad's ultimatum expired, the ADF repeatedly and heavily shelled apartment blocks, private homes and other buildings (including clearly marked hospitals) in Ain ar-Remmaneh, Karm az-Zeitoun and Bedaro in East Beirut between 10 February and 12 April, killing nearly 200 civilians and wounding over 350. The Maronites remained steadfast, though and held their positions, while the Syrians did not attempt an assault. Instead, they continued random shelling for days, then weeks and then months. Still, their pressure was not enough: convinced that the Israeli right-wing government of Prime Minister Menachem Begin was edging towards launching a military intervention in Lebanon, and in attempt to provoke exactly that and to expand the Phalangist sphere of influence further north, Bashir Gemayel and Samir Geagea led a commando force into the village of Ehden, south-east of Tripoli, on 13 June. After surrounding the place, the Phalangists assaulted the home of Tony Frangieh, son of the former president and commander of the ZLA. Apparently believing they were coming under attack from Muslim forces, Frangieh's bodyguards and villagers returned fire, wounding Geagea and sending his men into an orgy of violence. They broke into the property and massacred 33 people from Frangieh's clan, including Tony, his wife Vera and their young daughter.

The stench of revenge was now in the air. On 17 June, Suleiman Frangieh publicly announced that no Phalangist would be left alive in northern Lebanon. Seeing the assault as a direct offence against Syria, Damascus ordered the ADF into action, and on the early morning of 28 June, about 80 armed men wearing civilian clothes – actually special forces of the Syrian Arab Army – entered the Christian villages of al-Qaa, Ras Ba'albek, al-Jadida and al-Kakhah, and took 29 young women from their homes under the excuse that they would all be returned after questioning. Later the same day, Lebanese authorities were directed to the spot where bodies of 26 of the detainees – all killed by gunshots – were found in a mass grave.

Desperate, Gemayel and Chamouns called for a meeting with top ADF commanders in the headquarters of the Military Council on 1 July. During the conference – attended by Pierre Gemayel and Major General Khatib – Maronites began openly questioning the position and future of the ADF and explicitly blaming the Syrians for the al-Qaa massacre, although having no evidence for their involvement. However, the Syrians – supposedly convinced that this act was carried out as retaliation for the attack on Frangiehs in Ehden – not only formally refused to accept any involvement in, or connection with, the massacre, but even assisted in an investigation. The meeting ended inconclusively, but with the Phalangists determined to keep on their acts of provocation.

A 'technical' of the Phalange during street fighting in Beirut. The vehicle is a UNIMOG truck mounting a quad-barrel Soviet-made ZPU-4 14.5mm heavy machine gun. Most of the troops have Israeli-supplied helmets and flak vests. (Efim Sandler Collection)

A T-55 of the Syrian Army navigating the ruined streets of Beirut in 1978. (Albert Grandolini Collection)

headquarters at Saife and the NLP headquarters near the Ministry of Defence. Over 60 people were killed that day and more than 300 wounded. The bombardment continued for four days and hit three hospitals, including the Hotel-Dieu de France (which was demolished by 130 shells), the Saint Georges Hospital and the Geitawi Hospital. The rate of shelling sometimes reached one bomb per minute, and by 6 July, large parts of East Beirut were heavily damaged, with 160 civilians killed and over 500 wounded.

Indeed, only hours later, Gemayel and Chamouns ordered their units to start harassing the Syrians.

The spark that initiated the Hundred Days' War came at 1330 hours on 1 July, when two hand-grenades were thrown into the Amber Cinema, killing one soldier of the ADF and wounding five others. Later the same afternoon, Syrian military vehicles were fired at from cars passing by in the Ashrafieh district. Shaken, the Syrians made a controlled retreat to the line connecting the al-Amal newspaper building and the Beirut Bridge, although they had hardly reached there when they came under a new attack and had one of their BTR-152 APCs hit by a light anti-tank weapon and another by an RPG-7. In attempt to deter the enemy, Major General Khatib reacted in the usual fashion: at 1600 hours, Syrian units surrounded the Ain ar-Remmaneh district and blocked all entries and exits, before subjecting its predominantly Christian-populated suburbs to fire from tanks and heavy mortars. Without attempting to actually penetrate the suburb, the Syrians continued firing for five hours, eventually causing more damage to the district on that day alone than in the entire civil war since 1975. Some 35 Lebanese were killed and 88 wounded in the bombardment, most of them civilians. The defenders of Ain ar-Remmaneh were able to offer only minimal resistance to the attack.

On 2 July, the Syrians reinforced their shelling, this time adding Soviet-made M240 240mm mortars to hit not only Ain ar-Remmaneh, but also Hadath, Ashrafieh and Furn al-Chebbak. They first lightly bombarded the market area, to scare many of the Muslim merchants there into leaving for their homes in West Beirut. There followed a heavy barrage of the Phalange

ON THE BRINK[4]

By now, Prime Minister Begin's government was seriously considering a military intervention in Lebanon. Armoured and artillery units of the IDF were already amassing along the border, while, in a public demonstration for the Maronites, seven Israeli Aircraft Industries (IAI) Kfir fighter-bombers of the Israeli Defence Force/Air Force (IDF/AF) buzzed Beirut – shattering windows as they went – late on the afternoon of 6 July 1978. In the evening, Begin, Minister of Defence Ezer Weizman and other prominent Israeli officials made public statements to warn that Israel would 'not stand idle and watch the Christians being massacred'. General Shlomo Gazit, chief of the AMAN, the Israeli military intelligence service, said during a press conference: 'The immediate repercussions of the fighting in Lebanon, as far as we're concerned, are not really great. What does worry us is the very fact that one can crush systematically the Christian population just because they are a minority in the Middle East and nobody cares about their existence and their future.'

Syrian commandos, armed with (from left to right) an RPK machine gun, AKM assault rifle and RPG-7, searching for their opponents from the top of one of the tall buildings on the outskirts of East Beirut during the Hundred Days' War. (Albert Grandolini Collection)

A Syrian commando soldier with local civilians in West Beirut in 1978. (Albert Grandolini Collection)

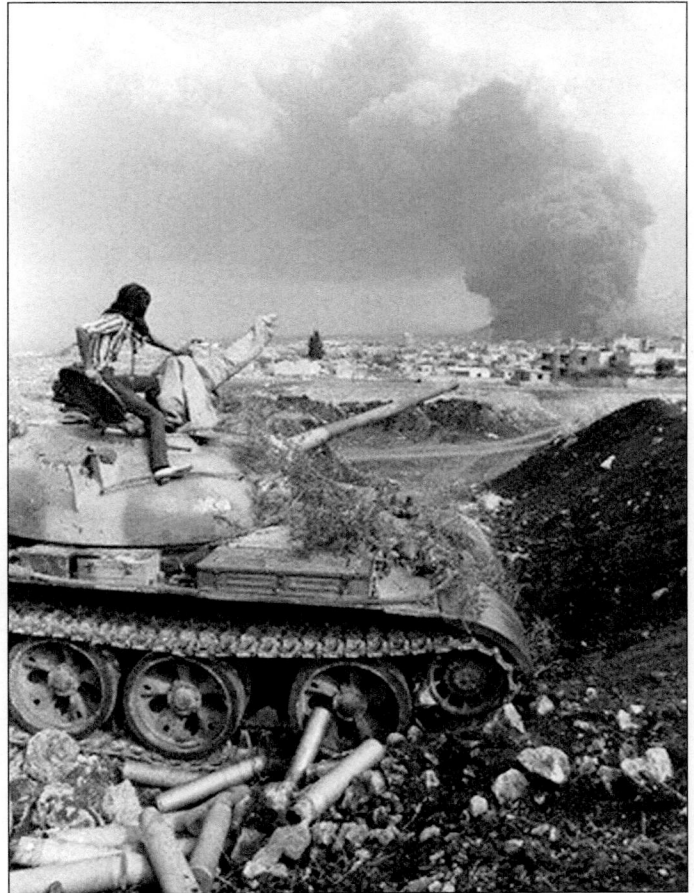

A Syrian T-62, seen against the backdrop of East Beirut, burning during the Hundred Days' War of 1978. (Albert Grandolini Collection)

This demonstration of power, and President Sarkis' threat of resignation, eventually had the desired effect: the Syrians stopped bombarding East Beirut. Arguably, this was less related to Israeli threats, which never particularly impressed Hafez al-Assad. The principal factor influencing his decision was that his troops had obviously failed to impose his ultimatum because of numerous military weaknesses. Not only was the SyAAF – careful to avoid provoking the superior IDF/AF – limited to sporadic demonstrative flights over East Beirut by its Sukhoi Su-20 fighter-bombers, but the artillery of the Syrian Arab Army proved hopelessly imprecise. Deployed with the help of only one forward artillery observer (positioned on top of the Rizk Tower), the artillery failed to score even one hit on either the Phalangist or NLP headquarters, both remaining fully operational throughout the barrage. Moreover, the Syrians failed to hit any of the first-floor tunnels constructed by the Christians between local buildings, which enabled them to freely manoeuvre their troops. Thus, the artillery effort failed to 'punish' what was now Syria's primary opponent in the country, the ADF's retaliation against the Phalange being a complete failure.

WAR BY OTHER MEANS[5]

Of course, Hafez al-Assad was not about to just let the Maronites get away. Better than anyone else, he knew that there were other means of exercising pressure upon them. None other than Bashir Gemayel – highly satisfied with getting the Israelis involved – was quick to provide him with a related provocation. On 31 July, the commander of the Phalange ordered a resumption of harassment of the ADF. Once again, this was staged from the Ain ar-Remmaneh district, but in a form that came as a tactical surprise for the Syrians. For the first time ever, the Phalange deployed French-made Milan anti-tank guided missiles (ATGMs), M50 Shermans and French-made M50 155mm howitzers – all only recently delivered from Israel – to target Syrian Army T-55s. Following quick consultations with Assad and Hikmat Chehabi, Chief-of-Staff of the Syrian Army, Major General Khatib reacted by resuming the shelling of ash-Shayah, Ain el-Remmaneh, Ashrafieh, Karantina, Furn ash-Shabak, Badaro and al-Hawtah: this went on for the next 12 days, killing and wounding dozens. To the international press, Chehabi explained his decision as 'logical': '[The] position of the Deterrence Forces in the locality of as-Sayda was attacked by 155mm howitzers and heavy machine guns, burning and wounding numerous soldiers. Thus, they were forced to respond with their organic weapons and have silenced the sources of fire.'

That said, once again the Syrian retaliatory fire proved next-to-useless militarily. Unsurprisingly, even Damascus became keen to renew negotiations with the Maronites. Consequently, on 10 August, an agreement was reached under which the ADF forces were to evacuate six buildings in three neighbourhoods of Ashrafieh and two bridges at the eastern entrance to East Beirut and were to be replaced by Sudanese troops. In the light of this humiliation, the Syrian strongman had his armed forces hit back at the Christians in a particularly demoralising fashion, by launching small-scale attacks on their distant strongholds in the north. By this point in the Lebanese Civilian War, the Maronites were often boasting about Mount Lebanon being their 'fortress': Assad was keen to demonstrate that they were wrong. Between 19 and 25 August, the Syrian contingent of the ADF attacked the town of Kour in the Batroun district, prompting nearly all of its population to flee. Between 24 and 26 August, Syrian troops of the ADF summarily executed 37 Christians in villages of Ainate,

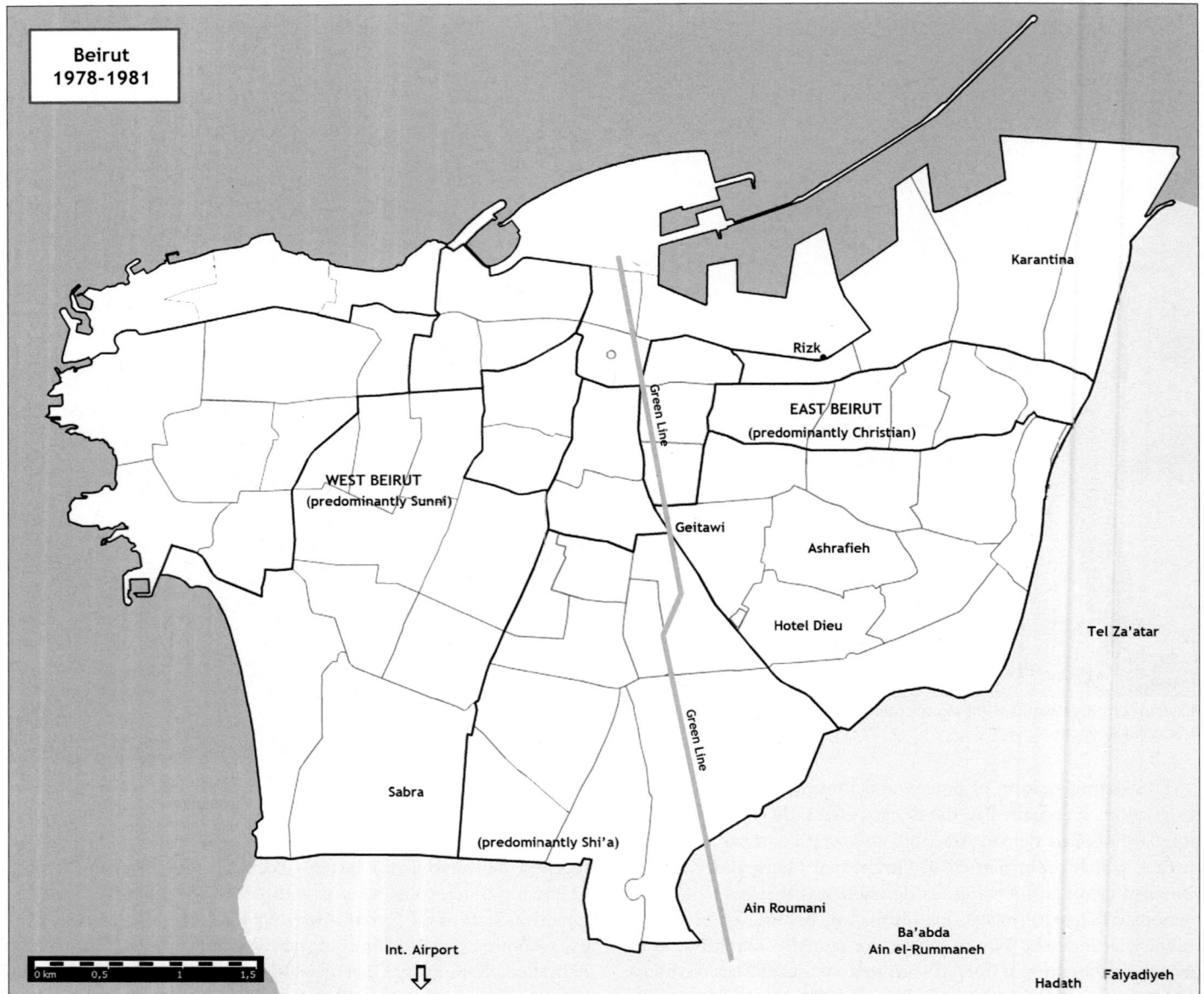

A map of the districts of Beirut. (Map by Tom Cooper)

Mshatiyyeh and Dayr al-Ahmar, and on 27 and 28 August they kidnapped six more from the town of Bcharre in northern Lebanon, killed them, burned their bodies and handed them over to local officials.

This time it was Bashir Gemayel's turn to be surprised: in shock and anger, he demanded an immediate and forthright Israeli military intervention. When Begin – meanwhile involved in finalising peace negotiations with Egypt at Camp David in the USA – refused, the young Maronite leader severed all ties with Israel. Although he renewed the contact only a week later, he did so with a special request: that the IDF conduct a thorough survey of the Phalange and its needs and help improve its combat effectiveness. About a week later, the Chief-of-Staff of the IDF, General Rafael Eitan, dispatched a group of officers to Lebanon to audit the Maronite militias and then help build up their combat capability, along with a complex of fortifications and obstacles protecting their positions. The only difference now was that henceforth, Gemayel would have to pay for all the arms his forces received.

US INTERVENTION

Eventually, Israel limited its military intervention in Lebanon in 1978 to the warships of the IDF/Sea Corps (Israeli Navy) sporadically shelling Syrian positions along the coast. Unsurprisingly, small-scale massacres of civilians in distant villages occurred. Correspondingly, Gemayel ordered his troops to commit further provocations, prompting the ADF to resume the shelling of East Beirut and its suburbs on 29 and 30 September. Indeed, this time the Syrians expanded the barrage to the eastern sectors of Mount Lebanon and the Christian enclave in Jounieh, killing more than 70 civilians and wounding over 300 more, in addition to causing a massive amount of damage. The Christians fired back with what was to hand – including SNEB launchers for 68mm unguided rockets taken from the stocks of the Lebanese Air Force (reportedly to 'great effect'), installed in packs of eight tubes on their technicals and fired by remote control. This time, the US government reacted with a demand for an international conference on Lebanon. Damascus promptly rejected this, describing the American demands as an intervention and complaining that Syria had not been consulted in this regard. The new round of fighting thus went on until 7 October, with the Christians attempting several attacks in the Karantina area (crucial to keep them connected to the port of Jounieh) and against the Beirut River bridges. Undertaken overcautiously, all were easily repelled – partly with the help of artillery barrages, but also with fire from the Rizk Tower – leaving all the bridges in Syrian hands. Throughout this time, the battering of East Beirut by Syrian artillery continued without respite, severely restricting all movement and – indirectly – preventing large-scale Christian operations. The holding of the Rizk Tower (where the Syrians installed multiple rocket launchers) and the construction of several firing positions for their tanks on the first floor made it extremely difficult for the Christians to manoeuvre on the streets below. The ADF also prevented the Phalangists from delivering supplies.

The situation began to change only on 8 October, when several mortar rounds hit the compound of the US Embassy in Beirut, wounding two US Marines and 11 Lebanese. US President Jimmy Carter, who had already proposed a UN-sponsored international conference on Lebanon and the restoration of authority to President Sarkis, then persuaded the UN Security Council to approve Resolution 436, which called for an immediate ceasefire and a speedy evacuation of all the wounded. Only then did both the Christians and the Syrians agree to accept the demands, and the fighting stopped, thus ending the Hundred Days' War. However, this was too late for far too many people: not only were over 400 Lebanese civilians and up to 150 Syrians killed, but more than 1,000 people were wounded. Worst of all, the fighting temporarily displaced between 150,000 and 250,000 civilians, emptying Beirut of nearly half its population, and demolished more than 60,000 buildings. Many of those forced to flee subsequently emigrated, never to return.

3
WAR OF ATTRITION

As of 1978, the IDF had a decade-long history of raiding selected targets in Lebanon, its early operations in the country having been undertaken either by its air force or special forces in cooperation with the air force or navy. During the following period, most Israeli operations were still launched in reaction to attacks into Israel and aimed to destroy infrastructure and damage morale. However, gradually, ever-larger ground units became involved, ranging from battalion- to brigade-sized task forces, and the situation eventually became reminiscent of the conflicts with Egypt and Syria during the years between the June 1967 and October 1973 Arab–Israeli Wars. Unsurprisingly, many Israeli veterans recalled the 1978–79 period as the 'War of Attrition (in Lebanon)'.

IMPROVEMENTS TO THE IDF ARMOURED CORPS[1]
After abandoning the practice of having brigades in which each battalion operated a different type of main battle tank, the IDF Armoured Corps was streamlined in 1974 and all but three brigades were re-equipped with one type: the exceptions were the 454th and 460th Brigades (of which the latter served as the School of Armour) and the 320nd Brigade, equipped with captured T-54s, T-55s and T-62s that were overhauled and upgraded to Tiran-4, Tiran-5 and Tiran-6 standards. During the same year, the IDF withdrew from service the remaining M50 and M51 Shermans and began actively exploring amphibious operations in cooperation with the IDF/Sea Corps. Over the following years, the equipment of tank battalions and brigades was further standardised, resulting in 18 brigades being equipped with M48/M60s, eight with upgraded Centurions

(locally designated the Sho't Kal when modernised through the introduction of the Continental AVDS-1790-2A diesel engine and the Allison CD850-6 transmission) and four with Tirans.

By the 1979–81 period, the IDF Armoured Corps experienced no fewer than four major improvements. One was the withdrawal from service of the remaining M51 Super Shermans, which were by then hopelessly obsolete. Another change was the introduction of so-called 'quality upgrades' to its fleet of US-made M48 and M60 and British-made Centurion MBTs. The third was the service entry of the brand-new and indigenously designed Merkava MBT (see box below for details) and the fourth was a major reorganisation prompted by Israel's withdrawal from Sinai in Egypt in the aftermath of the October 1973 Arab–Israeli War.

Most of the quality upgrades were undertaken in reaction to experiences from the October 1973 Arab–Israeli War and took time to introduce to service – but were in service by 1981. These included:

- Armour-piercing fin-stabilised discarding-sabot (APFSDS). The first Israeli-made APFSDS rounds were based on the US-made M735, with some improvements to increase their stability and penetration. They entered series production with Israeli Military Industries (IMI) in 1978 under the designation M111 or Hetz-6 (also known as DM23 in Germany).
- Main-Gun Stabiliser. In 1977–78, gun stabilisers were introduced on the M60 series of MBTs, converting them to the M60A1 RISE standard (locally known as Magach-6B; the first unit to receive M60s equipped with such modification being the 500th Armoured Brigade). The same improvement was then introduced to the older M60s, all the surviving examples of the M48 series of MBTs (locally known as Magach-3 and -5) and the remaining Centurions.
- Fire-Suppression System. On the basis of experiences from earlier conflicts, the IDF took care to acquire an automatic fire-suppression system for the crew and engine compartments of its MBTs. The first system to become available was developed by the Israeli company Spectornics, nicknamed SAFE, and introduced to service on Magach-6s in 1977–78.
- Engineering Equipment. In 1979, the IDF Ordnance Corps initiated several short-term projects aimed at developing – or adapting – obstacle-breaching equipment for available MBTs. The result was the development and acquisition of systems for mine-clearing with help of a line charge (Viper), mine-rollers (Nochri), ploughs and dozer kits in 1979–81.
- Explosive-Reactive Armour (ERA). Originally developed and patented in 1970 by German scientist Dr Manfred Held, ERA was designed to protect vehicles from shaped-charge projectiles and, if several layers were applied, sabot ammunition. The Israelis developed their first variant in 1975 – in a cooperation between the IDF and Rafael – nicknamed it Blazer (*Baltan* in Hebrew), and its application on operational Magach-6s and Centurions began in 1978. By 1981, all the active-duty M48/M60 and Centurion tanks were equipped with ERA (the addition of the gun stabiliser, a new fire-control system, the fire-suppression system and Blazer reactive armour on

A ceremony marking the first Merkava company achieving operational status, at Sindiana on 29 October 1979. (IDF)

Centurion MBTs resulted in the variant designated the Sho't Kal Gimel).

On 26 April 1979, the first four Merkava Mk 1s were handed over to Colonel Nati Golan during a modest ceremony at the MASHA 7100 Works of the Recovery and Maintenance Centre of the IDF. Golan, a recipient of the rarely issued Medal of Valour, Commander of the Tze'elim Training Base and newly appointed CO of the 7th Armoured Brigade, was then given the task of establishing the first unit equipped with the new tank in a temporary camp in the Negev Desert. This process was closely monitored by teams from both MASHA and the Tank Development Authority (RAPAT), in order to recognise any possible issues and react promptly. By the summer of 1979, the number of available Merkava Mk 1s increased to 11, and they were officially assigned to the 82nd Battalion of the 7th Armoured Brigade: following a major ceremony at the Sindiana firing range, the unit was declared operational and redeployed to the Golan Heights. That said, the 7th Armoured Brigade was fully equipped with Merkavas only by February 1982. Finally, in 1981, three units began receiving Merkava Mk 1s:

- 126th Battalion of the 211th Armoured Brigade
- 196th and 198th Battalions of the 460th Armoured Brigade (which continued functioning as the School of Armour)

Pending production of additional Merkavas, in 1979 the IDF placed an order for 200 M60A3 MBTs in the USA. Their delivery began in 1981, by when the Armoured Corps was already busy establishing and working up four additional reserve tank brigades (the 580th, 640th, 847th and 943rd). None of these were brought to their full nominal strength by 1982, though, and the same was true for two out of three tank brigades of the 252nd Division: its 14th and 401st Armoured Brigades still had only two tank battalions each. As before, the mass of the IDF's armoured brigades were reserve formations. Indeed, as of 1981, there were only six active-duty brigades:

- 7th, equipped with Merkava Mk 1s
- 188th, equipped with Sho't Kal Gimels
- 14th, 211th, 401st and 500th, all equipped with Magach-6Bs and Magach-6Rs

By the same time, only the two training tank brigades (460th and 844th) still operated a mix of different types, while the four reserve brigades (265th, 691st and 889th of the 440th Reserve Division and the 320th of the Northern Command) were equipped with three battalions of Tirans. Overall, by the end of 1981, the IDF Armoured Corps had a strength of 31 operational brigades and four training brigades, equipped with about 3,500 tanks of different types.

GLORIOUS TIMES[2]

For members of the IDF Artillery Corps, the period from 1974–80 is often referred to as the 'glorious period'. As described in Volume 1 of this work, during the October 1973 Arab–Israeli War, the Israelis learned the lesson that the artillery was one of most important branches of its ground forces, not just a supporting element, as previously thought. Correspondingly, in 1974, the Chief Artillery Officer, General Nati Sharoni, requested that his branch be expanded with 20 battalions of US-made M109 155mm self-propelled howitzers and submitted an order for 200 such vehicles, associated Alfa ammunition carriers and TPQ-

GENESIS OF THE MERKAVA

The widespread opinion that the Merkava tank project had been initiated because of the withdrawal of Great Britain from its joint venture with Israel related to the Chieftain tank is only partially true. Immediately after the June 1967 Arab–Israeli War, the government in Tel Aviv had recognised the need to sponsor the development of indigenously designed and manufactured military platforms – for its air force, for the armoured corps and for the navy of the IDF. In August 1967, Prime Minister Levi Eshkol – supported by Minister of Defence Moshe Dayan and Minister of Finances Ze'ev Sharef – approved the development of an indigenous fighter-bomber and main battle tank.

The idea of having their own tank had also been cooking within the Tank Branch of the Office of Chief Ordnance Corps, then headed by Lieutenant Colonel Yisrael Tilan. Once the Chieftain project was closed and Israel found itself on the receiving end of significantly increased US military support, in 1969, all the energy and passion of General Israel Tal – Head of the Tank Directorate (MANTAK) – was also rerouted in this direction. During a meeting of the ministers of defence and finances with the top brass of the IDF on 20 August 1970, a decision was taken to launch the 'Israeli tank' project. Initially, there were two options on the table:

- copy an existing design, or
- develop an entirely new tank, but based on available systems

Yisrael Tilan proposed to build a tank with a new hull but using the turret of the US-made M48/M60 series (nicknamed the *Magach* by the IDF) and the Continental diesel engine. Eventually, Chaim Bar-Lev, the IDF Chief-of-Staff, made the decision on 14 September 1970, concluding as follows: '[T]he tank will not be of a new generation, but based on the existing knowledge and parts, or those developed in two–three–four years from now, so by the end of the day the tank will be somewhat better than our existing M60 and M48A3, but including no revolution in armament or armour; still a good tank in the conventional group.'

The structure of the emerging Merkava Project (*Merkava* is Hebrew for 'Chariot', and was officially assigned in July 1970, although the project remained known as 'own tank' or 'Israeli tank' for years to come) was defined by the IDF Quartermaster Directorate as follows:

- MANTAK (Tank Directorate, headed by General Israel Tal): responsible for overall project management
- RAPAT (Tank Development Authority, headed by Colonel Yisrael Tilan): responsible for research and development
- MASHA 681 (Recovery and Maintenance Centre, headed by Colonel Mordechai Ron-Nes): responsible for production

Right from the start, the most famous feature of the Merkava was an engine installed in the front. The idea was proposed by Tilan as a solution to retain the versatility of the platform. Tal concluded that this fitted his own vision of offering better protection and would improve tactical mobility. Eventually, Tal managed to persuade all his opponents and get a green light for such a solution from his superiors, while Tilan then worked out all the technical details.

As mentioned above, all issues related to research and development were within the responsibility of Tilan's team. The main issue he next faced was the construction of a production line capable of rolling out about 100 tanks per year – and at a cost comparable to that of the US-made M60. His choices were to use one of the existing IDF plants, IMI or Urdan. Eventually, Tal decided to go for his own plant, with the IMI and Urdan to act as sub-contractors. The first computer-controlled machine for cutting metal for the tank was acquired from the Froriep company in West Germany, and a rotating station for handling turrets was purchased from France. By April 1971, the wooden mock-up had been finalised and Tilan proposed to build a testbed based on the Centurion MBT as a proof of the concept: essentially, the hull of this vehicle was cut and widened, and the Continental engine positioned in front. Its construction was completed in September 1971 in a cooperation between the Ordnance Corps and Urdan, while the mock-up of the turret was constructed by Nachmani Engineers, which was also responsible for the fitting of other systems.

By 1972, it became obvious that the originally planned 750hp Continental engine was insufficient, and a request was issued for the design of a 900hp engine: this became available on 1 July 1973, when the first prototype of the Merkava performed its maiden run on one of the Ordnance Corps' test ranges. However, all further work was frozen during the October 1973 Arab–Israeli War and for several months afterwards, and it was only in December 1974 that the final version of the first prototype – the 0001 vehicle – was ready for testing. Around the same time, a dispute developed between Tal and Tilan, prompting the latter to leave the project (and the IDF) in early 1975. Nevertheless, in the summer of the same year, the future plant for the new tank – MASHA 7100 (originally MASHA 681) in Tel Hashomer – was ready to launch production, and already involved in preparing the prototypes. Its newly appointed commander/director, Lieutenant Colonel Chaim Biran, still had doubts about actually running series production, and was thus sent to West Germany to visit the factory assembling Leopard MBTs near München and the hull-manufacturing plant outside Hamburg. Eventually, MASHA 7100 launched production of the first eight Merkavas in January 1976. On 18 May 1977, the office of the Minister of Defense proudly released the first information about its development and one image of the tank.

A Merkava Mk 1 at full speed during an exercise in October 1979. (IDF)

An M110 self-propelled howitzer seen during an exercise in 1981. By this time, the type was equipped with shells designed by Canadian artillery expert Gerald Bull, which enabled it to out range all artillery pieces in the Palestinian arsenal. (Photo by Yosi Elmakis)

A pair of M107 self-propelled howitzers on the Golan Heights in 1981. (IDF)

Not all the Israeli armament of the 1970s included the latest technology. A unique formation was the 9304th Anti-Tank Battalion. Established in 1974 from elements of the 755th Battalion, which operated obsolete SS-11s of French origin and captured Soviet-made 3M6 Shmel (ASCC/NATO-codename 'AT-1 Snapper') anti-tank missiles, the 9304th was equipped with about 20 BRDM-2 armoured cars, each mounting six 9M14 Malyutka (ASCC/NATO-codename 'AT-3 Sagger') anti-tank guided missiles. The unit saw no action before 1982 and was disbanded only two years later. (IDF)

37 artillery radars, while requesting that Washington also provide MGM-53 Lance tactical ballistic missiles. This equipment began arriving in 1975, together with immense stocks of ammunition, necessary to expand the war reserve. The new arrivals prompted a wholesale phasing-out of older inventory and the establishment of two major new units: the 9275th Battalion equipped with Lance and 418th Battalion with indigenously manufactured IMI MAR-290 Haviv MRLS systems.

By 1977, war stocks of the IDF Artillery Corps totalled about 1,200 rounds per tube of medium calibre, while a total of 450 M107A1, M109A1 and M110A1 self-propelled artillery pieces were delivered from the USA. Furthermore, domestic industry installed 72 155mm howitzers and 72 160mm mortars on the chassis of disused M4/M50/M51 Sherman tanks, creating self-propelled vehicles known as the Soltam L-33 and Soltam M-68. Towed artillery was not ignored: on the contrary, it was expanded with 48 M114 155mm howitzers from the USA, 36 captured Soviet-made M-46 130mm guns and 90 D-30 and M-38 122mm howitzers. Finally, the domestic industry expanded its ability to manufacture artillery ammunition from about 250 155mm shells per day in 1973 to more than 3,000 daily in 1975.

By the time that General Ben-David took over as Chief Artillery Officer in 1976, the Artillery Corps had been expanded from 26 battalions, three years earlier, to no less than 87 battalions. Ben-David thus paid special attention to training his gunners, improving their operational art and running joint exercises. As described in Volume 1 of this work, the primary problem of the entire IDF throughout this period, and so also its Artillery Corps, was the constant – yet critical – shortage of personnel. The initial solution was to reduce the number of units equipped with 120mm mortars, and convert these to heavy artillery systems: henceforth, medium mortar units became the responsibility of infantry and armour formations.

In 1980, Ben-David was replaced by General Arye Mizrachi, whose mindset was focused on timing, precision and concentration of firepower by all available means. During his tenure, the Artillery Corps introduced anti-personnel and anti-tank ammunition, and ran additional joint exercises, in order to improve precision while avoiding friendly losses due to the use of more powerful ammunition. Finally, the IDF Artillery Corps began introducing computers for fire-control calculations, RATAC and Cymbeline radars, and the first unmanned aerial vehicles (UAVs). Obviously, this was a step that prompted yet another reform of the training syllabus, and further increased requirements of artillery officers.

ELECTRIC HAWKS[3]

As described in Volume 1, during the years immediately following the October 1973 Arab–Israeli War, the primary 'iron fist' of Israel – its air force – was busy first with recovering from heavy combat attrition, and then with increasing its might. It expanded its fleet of McDonnell Douglas F-4E Phantom II interceptors and fighter-bombers, introduced to service the IAI Kfir fighter-bomber, nearly doubled the size of the fleet of McDonnell Douglas A-4 Skyhawk fighter-bombers and then acquired the McDonnell Douglas F-15A/B Eagle air superiority fighters. Finally, the IDF/AF began introducing attack helicopters as an intervention force and then greatly improved the firepower of its F-4E fleet through the introduction to service of precision guided munitions, including electro-optically guided bombs and missiles and new anti-radar missiles. Of course, new acquisitions and intensive training or replacement and then additional crews, went alongside an extensive review of doctrine, planning and strategy. Of particular importance were the massive improvements in the field of command, control and communication (C3) systems and the development of new tactics in reaction to numerous deficiencies revealed during the previous conflict, and the realisation that ground forces should never again be as reliant on the IDF/AF as they used to be. In the light of new threats, aerial warfare became much more complex and the air force was unlikely to be as free in its operations as during earlier wars.[4]

While some of the resulting concepts and the bolstered fleets of A-4s, F-4Es and Kfirs were put to the test during Operation Stone of Wisdom, the IDF/AF still found the time to consider its requirements for the future. Acquisition-wise, its primary problem during the second half of the 1970s was the exceptionally high price of the F-15: busy preparing all branches of the armed forces for a possible major war against several Arab opponents at once, the General Headquarters of the IDF considered quantity to be as important as quality, and thus opted to search for a new lightweight fighter-bomber as an alternative. Following extensive studies and flight-testing, the IDF/AF eventually decided to buy the General Dynamics F-16A/B Fighting Falcon. Negotiations had been underway since 1977, but the Carter administration conditioned their delivery to a successful conclusion of peace negotiations with Egypt. As soon as that treaty was signed, on 16 August 1978, the White House approved the sale of 75 new jets, comprising 67 single-seaters and eight two-seat versions.

The first groups of Israeli pilots and ground crews underwent conversion courses to the new type in the USA between November 1979 and October 1980, with first deliveries originally scheduled for 1981. However, in 1979, the 'Islamic' revolution in Iran swept Shah Mohammed Reza Pahlavi from power in Tehran, and the new government subsequently cancelled nearly all of its orders for weapons systems of Western origin, including that for 160 F-16A/Bs, 55 of which were in the process of assembly. Consequently, on 2 July 1980 Israel received its first Fighting Falcons (designated *Netz* or 'Hawk' in IDF/AF service) from the batch originally manufactured for Iran: all the other jets followed by the end of 1981.

There were many good reasons for the IDF/AF rushing the acquisition and then the service entry of the new type. The F-16 had been designed as a lightweight, uncompromised close-combat fighter, made to outfly and outfight the Soviet MiG-21. As such it won the Lightweight Fighter competition for the US Air Force in 1976 and was also ordered in large numbers by four major NATO partners in Europe. In comparison to the big and powerful F-15, its concept was remarkably simple: the smallest possible airframe was wrapped around the largest and most powerful possible engine to produce a modest wing loading and superior agility and manoeuvrability in combination with excellent endurance. It was slower, equipped with relatively austere avionics, and could carry a maximum of only six infra-red homing, short-range, air-to-air AIM-9 Sidewinder missiles – compared to a total of eight on the F-15 – in addition to the General Electric M61A1 Vulcan cannon installed internally. Nevertheless, thanks to major leaps forward in Western micro-technology in the 1970s, its APG-66 radar was still superior to comparable systems of Soviet origin. Ultimately, the F-16 was to prove exceptionally versatile and, before long, was to be developed into a multi-role 'heavyweight'.

Perhaps as the first indication of the qualities of the new type, and the priority its acquisition had received, the IDF/AF introduced it to service in a matter of a few months with three units that had previously each operated different types. The brand-new F-16A/Bs thus replaced the old Dassault Mirage IIICJ interceptors of No. 117 'First Jets' Squadron, the A-4 Skyhawks of No. 110 'Knights of the North' Squadron and the Israel-assembled Mirage Vs of No. 253 'Negev' Squadron.

ISRAELI NAVY OF 1978–81[5]

One of the most overlooked – and perhaps the most obscure – elements of the Lebanese Civil War was its naval component. To a certain degree, this might appear logical (at least at a first look), as the small Lebanese Navy played next to no role in the conflict. Indeed, even if Israel and Syria are added to the calculation, the naval element might appear to be a 'non-story' because the two sides' navies never clashed. Nevertheless, the war did have an important naval component, even if this primarily included small-

From left to right: a Sa'ar-4-class corvette, a Sa'ar-2-class fast missile boat and two Dabur-class patrol boats of the IDF/Sea Corps in 1978. (Clandestine Immigration and Naval Museum, Haifa)

A test launch of a Gabriel anti-ship missile from one of the first four Dvora-class boats, in the Red Sea in 1978. (IDF/Sea Corps)

INS *Aliya* with a Bell 206 helicopter on its rear deck. Clearly visible is the large hangar. The first helicopter landing on INS *Aliya* on the open sea was performed in September 1980. (Clandestine Immigration and Naval Museum, Haifa)

scale operations by relatively small vessels of Israel's navy.

The main role in the naval warfare off the Lebanese coast was played by the IDF/Sea Corps. Historically, and especially when compared to the IDF/AF, the service was never considered a 'high priority' branch, but in the late 1970s it was going through a period that was to shape its future well into the twenty-first century. The Israeli naval service entered the conflict in Lebanon having recently been involved in the War of Attrition against Egypt from 1967–70 and the October 1973 Arab–Israeli War. The War of Attrition had seen the introduction of guided anti-ship missiles to the Middle East, and events during its course had made it obvious that the IDF/Sea Corps could not effectively counter this threat. Over the following years, the service learned that it had to deal with the problem entirely on its own, with only minimal support from the IDF/AF. However, the improvements thus made became clear during the October 1973 War, from which the IDF/Sea Corps emerged as clearly superior to all of its opponents. The Syrian Navy had been strongly bolstered by deliveries of Soviet-designed vessels, while the Camp David Accords of 1978–79 and the subsequent withdrawal from Sinai significantly decreased Israel's 'strategic depth'. Israel also began facing 'maritime terrorism', for which its naval service was, once again, ill-prepared. All of this led to a complete reassessment of Israeli naval strategy, tactics and equipment in a process locally known as 'building the new force'.

The first improvements to address infiltrations from the sea were initiated in reaction to an event in 1975, when a Lockheed C-130 Hercules transport of the IDF/AF spotted the SS *Fakhr al-Din* as it was launching several boats for an infiltration 120km off the Israeli coast, and then guided the Israeli Navy's response. The Navy first decided to replace a number of observation points along Israel's northern coast with coastline surveillance stations, equipped with radars, including one inside southern Lebanon at Ras el-Bayada. This work was completed by 1978, by when the IDF/AF was reinforced through the introduction of three Rockwell Modell 1124 Westwind/IAI 1124N Sea Scan maritime patrol aircraft, equipped with the Litton AN/APS-504 radar in a bulbous nose radome, bulged observation windows and a pylon low on each side of the centre fuselage. As mentioned in Volume 1 of this work, all were operated by No. 120 'Desert Giants' Squadron of the IDF/AF, which reported to the 3rd Flotilla of IDF/Sea Corps' missile boats. Meanwhile, the naval base in Haifa underwent organisational changes aimed at enabling earlier detection and more effective intercepts, creating an echeloned defence, and the Navy established tight cooperation with the Air Force and amended its prevention-oriented tactics to one of offensive operations.

By 1979, the IDF/Sea Corps was massively expanding the firepower of its warships. Sa'ar-class missile boats were all gradually upgraded to deploy US-made RGM-84A Harpoon anti-ship missiles, in addition to the Israeli-made Gabriel Mk 2s, while they were also given the capability to target objects on the coast. By this time, two classes of very fast patrol boats armed only with machine guns were either entering service or were about to do so. The first of these were the Dabur-class boats, the first 22 of which were acquired from the USA, while 12 additional examples (Ben-Ami-class vessels) were constructed under licence by IAI Ramta.

The company subsequently developed an even more powerful type – the Dvora-class, which featured the latest technological solutions – but these were initially turned down by the IDF/Sea Corps, probably for cost reasons, as was the idea of arming them with Gabriel missiles.

The Israelis did not ignore the possibility of underwater infiltrations, two Sa'ar-2-class boats being modified through the addition of a variable-depth towed sonar acquired from the USA in 1979. During the same year, three additional enhancements were introduced to the service. The first was the addition of the General Dynamics Phalanx Close-in Weapons Systems (CIWS, based on the General Electric M61A1 Vulcan six-barrel gun) on all 12 Sa'ar-4-class missile boats then under construction, to improve their defences against anti-ship missiles and add to their firepower against small boats (the last Sa'ar-4, INS *Komemiyut*, was launched on 19 July 1979). The second enhancement was the installation of UGM-84A Harpoon anti-ship missiles on the Gal-class attack submarines (a process completed in 1983).[6]

Finally, the IDF/Sea Corps began introducing a ship-based helicopter capability. This project started with the attempt to fit unmanned Gyrodyne QH-50 DASH UAVs to Sa'ar-4-class vessels. However, the tests did not go well and the required development took much too long, prompting the Navy to switch to manned helicopters. Project Goldfinch, which ran from the mid-1970s, included the Sa'ar-4-class INS *Tarshish* being equipped with an improvised helipad and a hangar for Bell 212 helicopters. Two ships were subsequently constructed with an extended stern to accommodate a permanent hangar and a full-sized helipad: INS *Aliya* and INS *Geula*, commissioned in 1980 and 1981, and subsequently re-designated as the Sa'ar-4.5-class, the development of which was financed by the sale of two Sa'ar-4-class vessels to Chile in 1979. The Sa'ar-4.5-class ships had a corvette-sized hull with some structural improvements, a mixture of systems from the Sa'ar-4-class vessels and several new developments. The first two ships – both were frequently used as naval command posts – were followed by INS *Romach*, commissioned in 1981 without a hangar and helipad. This sub-class was then expanded through the addition of INS *Keshet* and INS *Nirit* in 1982 and 1983, respectively.

A Sa'ar-4-class corvette launching a RGM-84A Harpoon in 1977. (Clandestine Immigration and Naval Museum, Haifa)

NEW FORCE

The constantly increasing strength of the force, along with the withdrawal from Sinai and a change in threat nature, eventually prompted the IDF/Sea Corps into a major reorganisation – known as the 'New Force Concept'. In early 1979, its three major bases (Haifa, Ashdod and Eilat) assumed responsibility for the defence of their respective sectors to a depth of 30 nautical miles from the coastline. One implication of this decision was that all naval elements were divided between these bases and responded to local commanders – unlike previously when, for example, submarines of the 7th Flotilla reported directly to the IDF/Sea Corps commander, even if based in Haifa. In May 1979, the 11th Flotilla – originally based at Sharm el-Sheikh on the southern tip of the Sinai Peninsula – was relocated to Ashdod on the Mediterranean. By this time, all of its ships were in poor technical condition and in need of overhauls and upgrades, but none materialised. This change was assessed as making the chain of command more flexible, while improving cooperation.

To test the new organisation, the IDF ran a major branch exercise in October 1979 that simulated an attack on the Israeli coastline by 12 missile boats, two submarines and nine teams of naval commandos. The coastal defences, provided only by the IDF/AF and coastal observers, were completely over-run, exposing the inability of the Air Force to prevent naval attacks on Israel. This and other experiences eventually prompted the IDF/Sea Corps into intensive research about its future requirements. Its representatives and those of IAI, Rafael and Israel Shipyards also visited the USA, Italy, France and Germany in an attempt to gain a better understanding of the thinking and operations of other navies, and to learn technological aspects of modern naval warfare. Furthermore, the command of the force organised a number of discussion boards for its commanding officers to review the dynamics of the naval battlefield from the past and into the future. The result was a detailed document that summarised the mission of the IDF/Sea Corps, its assets and their application, which was presented by its new Chief-of-Staff, General Ze'ev Almog, to the Chief-of-Staff of the IDF, Rafael Eitan. On 30 September 1980, General Eitan reacted by approving the Navy's programme for building a new force that was to include 24 missile boats, six submarines, 30–40 patrol boats, four or five anti-submarine warfare ships, 14 maritime helicopters and eight landing craft, along with the acquisition of missile defence systems.

In 1982, a revised document was presented to the IDF Chief-of-Staff, including a requirement for 18 fast missile boats (with eight Sa'ar-4 and 10 Sa'ar-5 vessels), four submarines, six anti-submarine warfare vessels, 14 helicopters, 40 Dabur-class patrol boats and eight landing craft. This resulted in two conceptually new and ambitious projects: the Sa'ar-5-class corvettes and Dolphin-class submarines.

At 1,000 tonnes and with a crew of 60, the Sa'ar-5s were planned to become bigger

Another view of a test launch of a Harpoon from one of the Sa'ar-4-class corvettes. Barely visible at the base of the smoke column released by the booster-stage of the missile is the rear turret with its 76mm OTO Melara gun. (Clandestine Immigration and Naval Museum, Haifa)

Taken in Haifa during the visit by Egyptian President Anwar el-Sadat to Israel on 24 September 1979, this photograph shows one of the Osa-class fast missile boats of the Egyptian Navy in the foreground, together with a Sa'ar-2-class fast missile boat of the IDF/Sea Corps. (Clandestine Immigration and Naval Museum, Haifa)

Table 1: IDF/Sea Corps ORBAT, 1978		
Base	Unit	Equipment
C-in-C General Michael Barkai		
Directly subordinated: 13th Flotilla (naval commandos)		
Haifa	3rd Flotilla	23 missile boats (eight Sa'ar-4s, three Sa'ar-4.5s, six Sa'ar-3s, six Sa'ar-2 ASWs)
	7th Flotilla	three Gal submarines
	914th Division	patrol boats
Ashdod	11th Flotilla	INS Bat-Sheva, three Ashdod-class, three Kishon-class, five transports
	916th Division	patrol boats
	31st Division	fast missile craft (Sa'ar-4s)
Eilat	915th Division	patrol boats
	4th Flotilla	missile boats (Sa'ar-2/4s)

Table 2: IDF/Sea Corps ORBAT, 1981		
Base	Unit	Equipment
C-in-C General Michael Barkai		
Directly subordinated: 13th Flotilla (naval commandos)		
Haifa	3rd Flotilla	missile boats (eight Sa'ar-4s, three Sa'ar-4.5s, six Sa'ar-3s, six Sa'ar-2 ASWs)
	7th Flotilla	three Gal-class submarines
Ashdod	11th Flotilla	INS Bat-Sheva, three Ashdod-class, three Kishon-class, five transports
	Flotilla of Coastline Security	Dabur-class patrol boats
Eilat	915th Division	patrol boats

and more powerful vessels, eminently suitable for the combined battlefield concept right from its inception. The weapons system was to include 16 anti-ship missiles, an anti-aircraft system with 64 Barak surface-to-air missiles – with a dual purpose, because it had capability against small surface targets – two Phalanx CIWS, 10 anti-submarine torpedoes and a helicopter with anti-submarine warfare capability, supported by a passive towed sonar assemblage. The projected maximum speed was still high, at 34 knots, but the range was limited to about 2,000km. The propulsion system – based on a combined diesel or gas (CODOG) concept – was to provide a cruising speed of 17 knots. Following two years of shaping the requirements and related research and development, the project was approved by the General Headquarters of the IDF and forwarded for a review to the Ministry of Defence in 1982.

While the Sa'ar-5 project was quite logical in the sense of expected future necessities, considering the previous decade of combat experience, the need for the Dolphin-class submarines was less obvious. Unsurprisingly, both projects found no support from the Ministry of Defence and experienced a significant dose of expected and unexpected delays. Eventually, the Israeli Navy's order of battle (ORBAT) as of 1978–81 was as provided in Tables 1 and 2.

SEABORNE INFILTRATION ATTEMPTS
Soon after the end of Operation Stone of Wisdom, it became clear that it had ended in failure. During the enterprise, the IDF deployed two task forces (one from the 36th Division and the other from the 96th Division), with about 7,000 infantry, paratroopers, a few armoured formations, plus engineers and artillery, to push the Palestinians away from the border. However, not only did the

mass of the militants evade the Israeli advance, but the operation did not go deep enough to prevent the Palestinians from being able to continue rocketing and shelling northern Israel or launching infiltration raids. But worst of all, the IDF never really withdrew from Lebanon after the offensive: supposedly on the initiative of Major Haddad of the SLA, it very much remained present, even if in a limited fashion, in the form of manned outposts on Lebanese territory. The peacekeeping UNIFIL forces had also failed in their mission – not only being unable to force the Israelis into an unconditional withdrawal, but also failing to keep the Palestinians away from the border. Before long, the Palestinians would renew their infiltration raids.

Indeed, only days after the end of Operation Stone of Wisdom, Israeli intelligence received the first reports of Fatah preparing a new seaborne attack from a training camp near Dahr el-Borj. Having experienced what damage such assaults could cause on at least two earlier occasions – in March 1975 and again three years later (see Volume 1 for details) – the IDF/Sea Corps began planning a pre-emptive operation. Drafted by the commandos of the 13th Flotilla, the enterprise was already in the advanced stages of training when the Chief-of-Staff of the IDF, General Eitan, decided to switch the mission's objectives and assigned the task to the paratroopers of the 35th Parachute Brigade. Operation Fall (Shaleket) was thereafter launched on 8 June 1978 by a party of naval commandos and paras led by Colonel Amnon Lipkin-Shahak, who embarked on one of the Sa'ar-class missile boats, which took them near their objective, about 45km north of the border. The landing was delayed as the scout party could not confirm having found the right spot, and then the paratroopers experienced problems during their transit by boat to the shore. Once ashore, Lipkin-Shahak decided to change the plan and deploy the commandos for a flanking attack, and they and the paratroopers eventually went in without synchronising their moves. Each force moved from building to building, searching them before setting demolition charges. A building found to be full of civilians was skipped, but the paratroopers then came under enemy fire while trying to demolish the next building: a bullet detonated the charges, killing two officers of the 50th Parachute Battalion. Hearing about this catastrophe, General Eitan ordered the immediate withdrawal of all the involved units. The paratroopers could not leave without the bodies of the two fallen soldiers, and thus a frantic effort was initiated to recover them from under the rubble. This bought time for Fatah militants to recover and stage a counterattack in which several Israelis were wounded. Nevertheless, the paras – supported by naval commandos – eventually managed to get back into their boats and escape into the darkness. While Operation Fall was proclaimed a success because most of the targeted

The *Agios Demetrios*, abandoned shortly before it was sunk in 1978. (Clandestine Immigration and Naval Museum, Haifa)

INS *Achziv* (P-63, left) and INS *Ashdod* (P-61) off Sharm el-Sheikh in 1978. (Clandestine Immigration and Naval Museum, Haifa)

bases were destroyed, there was no denying the loss of two men killed and eight wounded, and that Eitan had messed up by interfering in the planning for the mission and overruling the commanders of the IDF/Sea Corps. Ironically, the result was that the commander of the 13th Flotilla was removed from his post.

SKUNKS

Undeterred by this chaotic raid, Fatah was soon back preparing another infiltration. Late on 26 August 1978, one of the observation stations along the coast detected a 'skunk' – codeword for a suspicious surface object – and directed Dabur-class patrol boat 895 from the 914th Flotilla to investigate. The vessel quickly reached the scene and turned on its searchlight, only to find two men on a paddle boat powered by a small engine, loaded with weapons. Instead of opening fire, the skipper of the patrol boat performed a sharp manoeuvre that caused the tiny craft to flip over: both Palestinians were then picked up from the water and taken into custody.

The next Fatah operation proved much more complex. In September 1978, SS *Agios Demetrios*, a merchantman under a Cypriot flag and homeported at Larnaca, sailed from the port of Latakia in Syria to Tripoli in Lebanon before continuing its voyage through the Suez Canal to the Red Sea. Early on 30 September, the vessel reached the Straits of Tiran, where it was detected by

the Israeli observation posts at Sharm el-Sheikh. For reasons that are unclear, the observation post failed to identify the ship and declared it a skunk, but no move was undertaken against it before the vessel moved north, and contact was then lost. At about 1000 hours local time, the officer on duty responsible for the Red Sea Territory of Operations requested the landing ship INS *Ashdod* (P-61) to move out and relocate the skunk. Eventually, the *Agios Demetrios* was detected about 40km north of Sharm el-Sheikh, and the *Ashdod* approached to within about 200 metres, trying to communicate with the crew. When there was no response, and despite the rough seas, the Israeli amphibious vessel closed to within 50 metres and its crew fired warning shots into the air and the sea across the bow of the merchant ship. With this still prompting no reactions, permission was requested to board the ship. The officer on duty communicated this to the IDF/Sea Corps headquarters, and reported that the *Agios Demetrios* was on a 'black list' of ships likely to be used for a terror attack. However, intelligence officers in the headquarters refused to believe the duty officer and recommended leaving the vessel alone to prevent an international incident. Eventually, no less than the Chief-of-Staff of the IDF/Sea Corps, General Barkai, decided to proceed with the interception.

In the meantime, the Sa'ar-4-class missile boat INS *Reshef* was rapidly approaching the *Agios Demetrios*. With there still being no

A boat used by Palestinian militants to attempt an infiltration in August 1978. (Clandestine Immigration and Naval Museum, Haifa)

response from the crew, Barkai authorised the crew to target the bow of the ship with small-arms fire. The skipper of INS *Ashdod* then ordered his crew to hit cargo containers on the side of the merchantman with their machine guns: immediately afterwards, the *Agios Demetrios* turned sharply towards INS *Ashdod*, forcing the latter to cease fire and manoeuvre to avoid being struck. Now 200 metres away, the captain of the amphibious ship ordered his 20mm automatic cannons to open fire, and these sprayed the bow and the bridge, setting one of the cargo containers on fire. The conflagration caused one of the hidden rockets aboard to fly out in the direction of the *Ashdod*. Moments later, the *Agios Demetrios* crew began waving white cloths to indicate their intention to surrender. Naval commandos then quickly boarded the merchantman, detained the crew, extinguished the fire and turned the vessel back towards Sharm el-Sheikh. Subsequent inspections discovered 25 barrels filled with TNT and prepared for detonation, and it transpired that the entire 'crew' apart from the ship's captain were members of Fatah and on their way to attack Eilat. They first intended to open fire from a 122mm multiple rocket launcher hidden between cargo containers, then to disembark and flee to nearby Saudi Arabia, while setting off the *Agios Demetrios'* deadly cargo.

The headquarters of the IDF/Sea Corps ordered the skipper of INS *Ashdod* to take the captured merchant ship under tow to Eilat. Determined not to endanger his men, the Israeli captain requested INS *Reshef* to sink the vessel instead. The crew and the boarding party were evacuated and the two Israeli warships then moved to a distance of about 5,000 metres. At 1125 hours, the missile boat opened fire with its OTO Melara 76mm automatic gun and one

of the shells scored a direct hit on the barrels loaded with TNT, causing a fierce explosion that ripped apart the *Agios Demetrios*. What was left of the vessel sank within a matter of seconds.

OPERATION WHITE SWAN

Amphibious warfare vessels of the Israeli Navy were soon in action again. During the night of 5/6 October 1978, the IDF/Sea Corps dispatched two Kishon-class landing ships – INS *Etzion Gever* (P-51) and INS *Caesarea* (P-53) – escorted by missile boats and patrol boats, to the coast of Lebanon, south of Beirut. Each of the landing vessels carried one Magach-6B MBT recently modified through the installation of a gun stabiliser. Approaching to about 1,000 metres from the shore, the *Etzion Gever* and *Ceasarea* opened their front doors and the tanks then opened fire with their 105mm guns at a building identified as the local Fatah headquarters. The target was hit by the first few rounds, but both vessels drew heavy fire in return, prompting escorting boats to join the firefight. After an exchange of fire lasting 15 minutes, all Israeli ships were ordered to withdraw. This operation – codenamed White Swan (*Barbur Tzakhor*) – was also declared a success, despite its extremely dangerous set up that could have easily resulted in a catastrophe: lowering the front doors of amphibious ships on the open sea was against all safety regulations, especially considering the tilting of the vessels, only 36-metre-long, whenever one of the tanks fired its main gun. Unsurprisingly, this remained the sole enterprise of this kind ever attempted by the Israelis.

OPERATION LAMP

On 11 January 1979, three members of the DFLP infiltrated Israel near the village of Zar'it. The IDF detected their traces the following morning and launched a large-scale search operation but found nothing until one of the militants was spotted in the town of Ma'alot two days later. It turned out that a well-armed group was hiding inside a local guest house. Israeli forces attacked and shot them all, but not before a female civilian was killed after falling out of a window while trying to escape. In retaliation for this attack, the IDF launched Operation Lamp (Menora) on 18 January, based on intelligence received by Unit 504 from one of Fatah's commanders about the combatants and bases under his control deployed in the area between Hama Arnoun and Nabatiyah, in central southern Lebanon, north of the Litani River. With this intelligence being confirmed through cross-examination, the IDF decided to raid the PLO's positions in the area north and west of the Crusader fortress Beaufort Castle.

For Operation Lamp, the Northern Command of the IDF created two formations:

- Parachute Task Force: the 202nd and 890th Parachute Battalions and a Reconnaissance Unit of the 35th Parachute Brigade (commanded by Colonel Amnon Lipkin-Shahak) were to block the Arnoun area and destroy artillery and bunkers near Beaufourt Castle
- Golani Task Force: the 12th and 13th Infantry Battalions and the Reconnaissance Unit of the 1st Golani Infantry Brigade, commanded by Colonel David Katz, were to drive further north to the villages of Eishiah, Mahmoudiyeh and Mazra'at al-Qurayyah and destroy the local Palestinian bases and positions

Operation Lamp was initiated by the 202nd Parachute Battalion (commanded by Shaul Mofaz) moving out of the village

TOP SECRET: PART 1

In 1974, Israel secretly started supplying Christians with arms and ammunition. Organised by Mossad, the Israeli foreign intelligence service, and always run as 'top secret' operations, initial shipments included only firearms, always deposited at a pre-selected place inside Lebanon and then being picked up by the militants without an actual handover. Proper channels were established only in 1976, and then arms and ammunition were delivered directly from IDF stocks, before the cooperation was expanded to the training of Christian militiamen in Israel. Prime Minister Begin openly confirmed the links in 1977, soon after taking over and Israel became involved in fighting in southern Lebanon. In September of that year, the IDF ran its first joint operation with the SLA's Major Haddad. On 3 March 1978, the PLO captured a stock of Israeli-supplied weapons, including ex-IDF M50 Shermans and M3 halftracks. From around that time, Mossad began supplying the Phalange by sea, usually through the supply ship INS *Maoz*, which towed pontoons and barges and unloaded them at the mouth of the Nahr Ibrahim River – always under the protection of several warships. On 20 April, two landing ships of the 11th Flotilla, escorted by Dabur patrol boats of the IDF/Sea Corps, delivered trucks and ammunition to Gemayel's headquarters in Jounieh, north of Beirut. Four such deliveries – Operations Fence Bust and Leather Thread – were completed by the end of the year, after which the Phalangists began using their own landing craft and barges to take their troops for training in Israel. After the port of Jounieh was expanded in 1979, larger amphibious vessels of the IDF/Sea Corps were used to haul heavier equipment.[8]

Palestinians inspecting an M50 Super Sherman, captured from the Phalange on 3 March 1978. The vehicle was sprayed in two shades of grey overall and carried a full set of instructions in Hebrew inside. (AP)

of al-Qulayah towards Hama Arnoun, crossing the Litani River and positioning itself to wait for the rest of the Parachute Task Force. The 890th Battalion (commanded by Ze'ev Tzel) followed the 35th Brigade's Reconnaissance Unit (commanded by Moshe Ya'alon), which moved out of Dayr Mimas, crossed the Litani and split into three raiding parties in the direction of Yohmor, Beaufort and Arnoun. Acting quickly, the 202nd Battalion cleared Hama Amoun, demolishing several houses in the process, while the 890th Battalion overran several artillery and mortar positions near Beaufort Castle, blew up an ammunition bunker and took one prisoner. The Parachute Reconnaissance Unit, meanwhile, found and demolished one communication facility. With its task completed, the Paratrooper Task Force withdrew to a pickup point and was then evacuated by three Sikorsky CH-53 helicopters.[7]

The Golani Task Force moved out from Marjayoun, crossed the Litani River and then split into four parties. The 12th Battalion (led by Dov Gazit) advanced on Mahmoudiyeh, while the 13th Battalion (commanded by Yakov Sela) moved on Mazra'at al-Qurayyah. Meanwhile, one part of the Reconnaissance Unit (commanded by Giora Inbar) attacked Eishiah, and the other (under its deputy commander, Yaron Vinograd) moved north to block any possible intervention from that direction. The 12th Battalion cleared Mahmoudiyeh after a short firefight and demolished four buildings. The 13th Battalion encountered no opposition and completed its task by mining the area. The Reconnaissance Unit ran into several Palestinian positions in the Eishiah area, shot-up technicals mounting machine guns and demolished the road leading to the stronghold. Having completed all its tasks, the Golani Task Force withdrew back across the Litani River to Marjayoun.

Operation Menora was assessed as reaching all of its objectives: indeed, Minister of Defence Ezer Weizmann and IDF Chief-of-Staff General Eitan were pleased with its results and the performance of the units. The two task forces suffered just two men lightly wounded: in return, they reported about 30 Palestinian militants killed, 10 buildings demolished and the destruction of five artillery pieces and two technicals. Fatah subsequently confirmed 21 killed – including five Lebanese civilians – and eight buildings destroyed.

4

BEGIN DOCTRINE AND THE CAMP DAVID ACCORDS

During the following months, the attention of all involved parties focused on peace negotiations between Egypt and Israel, which led to the Camp David Accords, the first of a pair of which was signed on 17 September 1978; the second – a peace treaty between Egypt and Israel – was concluded on 26 March 1979. The two agreements caused shock and a fundamental change in Middle Eastern politics, especially in regards of the perception of Egypt – then the country with most powerful of the Arab armed forces, a history of leadership in the Arab world and a tradition of having more leverage than any other Arab state with advancing Arab interests. The decision of President Anwar el-Sadat to stop fighting Israel, accept its existence and normalise relations in exchange for a complete return of the Sinai under Egyptian control caused the disintegration of a united Arab front in opposition to Zionism, and a power vacuum in the Arab world which several local leaders – foremost among them Hafez al-Assad in Syria and Saddam Hussein in Iraq – attempted to fill. Moreover, the accords were seen as a virtual slap in the face by the majority of Arabs: feeling snubbed, they reacted with strong opposition to the Egyptian

Sadat (left) with Begin (right) and US President Jimmy Carter at Camp David in 1978. (CIA)

(From left to right) Israeli legal advisor Aharon Barak, Menachem Begin (both on the sofa), Anwar Sadat and Israeli Defence Minister Ezer Weizman during negotiations at Camp David in September 1978. (CIA)

decision, and isolated and excluded the country from the Arab League for many years.

WAR AT SEA

The PLO opposed the Camp David Accords, for not only were Palestinians excluded from the negotiations, but even the United Nations – the very creator of Israel – was not involved, and thus issues like the right to return, of self-determination and national independence and sovereignty of the Palestinians – the very core of the Arab–Israeli conflict – all remained unresolved. Unsurprisingly, after an interruption of a few months, the PLO resumed its infiltration attempts. In the spring of 1979, warships of the IDF/Sea Corps intercepted two vessels carrying infiltrators from Lebanon. On 3 March, INS *Ga'ash* (a Sa'ar-3-class vessel) caught the merchant ship *Ginan* with 10 Palestinian militants on board, about 55km west of Damour. On 28 March, the Sa'ar-2 class INS *Eilat* stopped and seized the merchantman *Stephanie*, with five militants and a load of weapons and explosives on board.

Signalling its disagreement with the Camp David Accords, the PLO then attempted to strike at both of the signatories. On 19 April, a box of cigars exploded at Cairo's main post office, killing a female customs inspector and wounding four others. A group naming itself the 'Eagles of the Palestinian Revolution' – actually a Fatah front – claimed responsibility. The next strike followed within 48 hours. Late on 21 April, Israeli coastal surveillance posts failed to spot a small motorboat moving in heavy seas. Four Fatah militants thus managed to reach the coast of Nahariya with a mission to take hostages and extract them to Lebanon. They broke into an apartment building and murdered a 4-year-old-girl and her father, before being caught by the police. In the ensuing gun battle, one policeman and two militants were killed, four civilians wounded and the two surviving gunmen taken prisoner.

Although Fatah – and thus the PLO – subsequently claimed all responsibility for these two actions, in Israel the infiltration into Nahariya triggered a public outburst of accusations against the IDF – and the Sea Corps in particular. The Palestinians were merely buying time. Realising that they could no longer count on support from Egypt, and that they had to expect Israel would now concentrate all of its military power upon their positions in Lebanon, both regular units and militias of the PLO adapted their tactics. Instead of launching additional infiltration attempts, they began fortifying their main bases in Lebanon. Major facilities had bunkers for their command posts and shelters for personnel. Moreover, both such installations and 'regular' units of the PLO had their air defences significantly bolstered through the acquisition of Soviet equipment. Among the latter were 9K32 Strela-2 man-portable air defence systems (MANPAD; ASCC/NATO-codename 'SA-7 Grail'), towed ZU-23 anti-aircraft guns and ZSU-23-4 Shilka SPAAGs. By 1981, these were bolstered through the service entry of even more powerful, mobile

The Dabur-class patrol boat with hull number 866, assigned to the 914th Flotilla, seen in 1978. (IDF/Sea Corps)

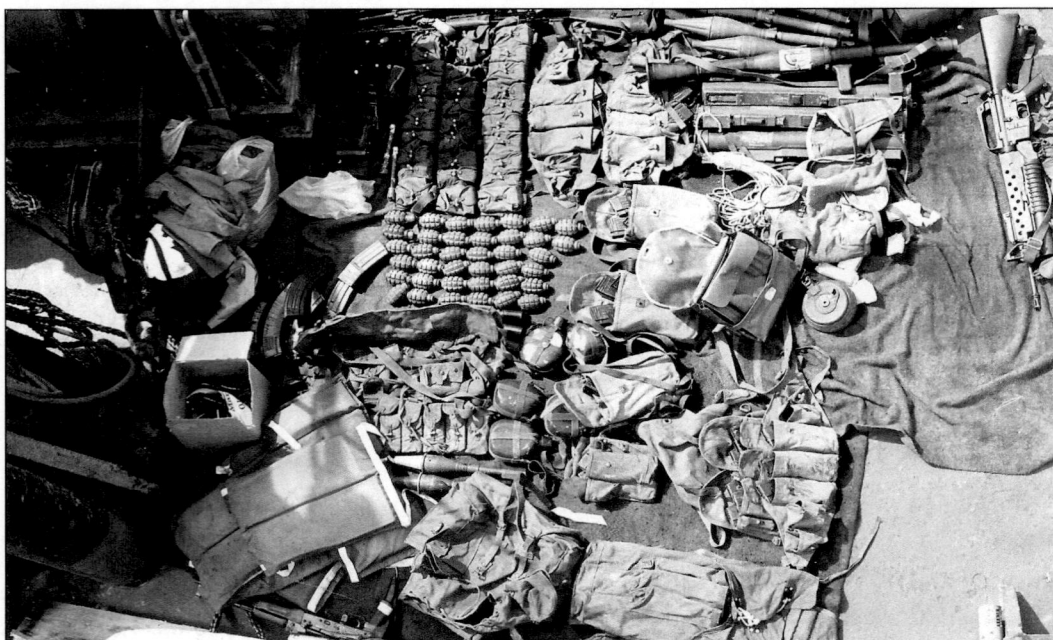

A weapons cache including AK-47/AKM assault rifles, RPG-7s, rifle-grenades, hand-grenades, mines, explosives and other gear captured aboard the merchant ship *Stephanie* on 28 March 1979. (Clandestine Immigration and Naval Museum, Haifa)

al-Assad refused to become involved.[1]

A few days later, the IDF launched a 'silent' raid on the port of Sidon, which was being used by the Palestinians. Two combat divers were deployed by a fast attack boat, and they positioned mines on the selected vessel before being safely evacuated. The mines detonated the following morning, but it turned out that they sank the wrong ship – even though this was also used by the PLO. The 'right' target was subsequently traced to the port of Tyre and sunk in another similar operation. Undeterred, the IDF/Sea Corps ran another retaliatory raid. Operation Scion was originally planned to include elements of the 35th Parachute Brigade, but its involvement was eventually cancelled and the raiding party included only naval commandos and one officer from Unit 504. Late on 17 May, the Israelis landed on Adloun beach, marched to their target to launch the attack, killed several occupants, demolished the main building and withdrew without suffering casualties, despite coming under heavy fire.

This operation drew a Palestinian response, when on 30 May a Dabur-class patrol engaged a speedboat equipped with a multiple rocket launcher and moving in the direction of Haifa. On 4 June, the Ras el-Bayada surveillance station spotted a small vessel some 2,500 metres from the coast and guided INS *Ga'ash* to investigate. The crew of the *Ga'ash* could not find anything at first, but after improved coordination with the ground station it detected a lone swimmer with a floating mattress – loaded with weapons – and quickly neutralised the threat.

BEGIN DOCTRINE

In early June 1979, only months after concluding the peace treaty with Egypt, Begin announced his new doctrine, under which Israel would henceforth not only retaliate to terrorist attacks, but proactively search to prevent them – through preventive military action – both against terrorist bases and weapons proliferation. Always carefully monitoring developments in Israel, officers of the Military Intelligence Directorate (MID; also Military Intelligence Division) of the Syrian armed forces promptly issued a warning. However, although the MID's commander, Ali Duba, reported directly to Hafez al-Assad, his voice was never as influential nor

9K31 Strela-1 infra-red homing surface-to-air missiles (ASCC/NATO-codename 'SA-9 Gaskin'), installed on the chassis of BRDM-2 armoured cars. Around the same time, the PLO worked out a number of unofficial rules with the UNIFIL peacekeepers, including permission to reposition at least 700 combatants within southern Lebanon and a number of agreements that granted it the right to run additional infiltration attempts virtually undisturbed.

Meanwhile, public criticism of the IDF/Sea Corps prompted the service to hit back at the PLO. On 22 April 1979, INS *Tarshish* and INS *Ga'ash* (both Sa'ar-3-class ships) deployed Gabriel missiles to hit two targets in Lebanon. The following day, INS *Eilat* and INS *Mivtach* repeated the exercise, and on 24 April, INS *Tarshish* and INS *Ga'ash* attacked again. Also on 24 April, the Israeli Air Force flew its first strike against PLO bases in southern Lebanon in years, while additional air strikes were undertaken on 6, 8, 23 and 24 May. Heavily hit, the Palestinians complained to Moscow and demanded action from Damascus, hoping for the SyAAF to stop the Israeli aerial onslaught. For the time being, though, Hafez

as powerful as the Air Force Intelligence Directorate (AFID; commanded by Muhammad al-Khuli). Moreover, not only were both the MID and the AFID already preoccupied with the growing crisis inside Syria, but the MID's assessment that the Israelis, once free of the threat from Egypt, would focus on fighting Syria and the PLO was 'lost' in the flood of other, apparently 'more urgent' reports. Subsequent Israeli actions thus did not take Damascus and the Syrian armed forces by surprise, but when they took place, they did cause a shock due to their severity.[2]

Only hours after Begin's announcement, McDonnell Douglas RF-4E Phantom II reconnaissance fighters of the IDF/AF – and Kfir C.2s equipped with specially configured noses containing reconnaissance cameras – flew the first in a series of regular photoreconnaissance missions over Lebanon. The more sorties were flown, the bolder the Israelis became, and before long they were not only regularly violating the sovereignty of a neighbouring nation, or making overflights over PLO bases and positions and those of other parties involved in the Lebanese Civil War, but also over positions of the Syrian contingent of the ADF. In turn, this violated yet another, little-known agreement, negotiated through US mediation in 1974 and again in 1976, under which Israeli military aircraft were not supposed to fly north of a line approximately between Tyre and Hasbaya, while Syrian military aircraft were neither supposed to fly south of the same line nor to strike targets in Lebanon.[3]

To an uninvolved observer, such an agreement was unlikely to mean a lot. However, to the Syrians, it made sure that their troops deployed with the ADF in Lebanon need not fear any sudden air strikes, and that their capital – a mere 30–40km further east – was safe from a sudden attack from the west. The Israeli decision to violate this agreement meant that they could not be trusted not to carry out such strikes, and henceforth, whenever Israeli jets did violate Lebanese airspace from the south or west, the SyAAF would scramble at least a pair of its own interceptors – and more often four – from one of its bases close to the Lebanese border. For a while at least, the two air forces played a game of cat and mouse: for several days, reconnaissance jets of the IDF/AF made ever deeper forays into Lebanese airspace, and the Syrians were getting their MiG-21 interceptors airborne. However, both sides were cautious enough not to risk an engagement.

SYRIAN ARMED FORCES OF 1979

As described in Volume 1 of this work, the reconstruction and subsequent build-up of the Syrian armed forces after the October 1973 Arab–Israeli War proved not only excessively costly but experienced a rude interruption when the USSR imposed an arms embargo in reaction to Syria siding with the Lebanese Christians and fighting the PLO in June 1976. Full relations between Damascus and Moscow were re-established only during a visit by Hafez al-Assad and his Minister of Defence Mustafa Tlass to the Soviet Union in April 1977. Even then, the Soviet leadership – presided over by Leonid Ilyich Brezhnev, who considered himself responsible for provoking the crisis that led to the catastrophic defeat of multiple Arab armed forces during the June 1967 War with Israel – remained keen to prevent a major conflagration in the Middle East. Therefore, Brezhnev refused to bolster the Syrian capability to strike at Israel: instead, he insisted on strengthening the country's defences through sales of largely obsolete equipment. For example, Moscow turned down all requests for the latest T-72 main battle tanks and Mil Mi-24 helicopter gunships and agreed to sell only 20 MiG-21bis interceptors, between 28 and 30 MiG-23MF interceptors, 20 of the Mach 2.3-capable MiG-25 interceptors, eight MiG-25RB reconnaissance fighters and equipment for 50 additional units equipped with surface-to-air missiles. All of this weaponry was defensive by nature: it was only thanks to an up-front payment in cash from Baghdad – where the Iraqi government was keen to initiate negotiations for a union with Syria – that the strike-capability of the Syrian Arab Air Force was bolstered through the acquisition of 36 additional MiG-23BN fighter-bombers. Brezhnev remained unmoved even once the Syrians – thanks to Saudi connections and funding – sponsored an acquisition of French-made Aérospatiale SA.342 Gazelle helicopters armed with AS.12 and HOT (High-subsonic, Optical, Remote-Guided, Tube-launched/ *Hautsubsonique Optiquement Téleguidé Tiré d'un Tube*) anti-tank guided missiles for the SyAAF in 1978.[4]

Moreover, even once related contracts were signed, the Soviets continued dragging their feet, usually offering the reason of the 'incompetence' of Syrian pilots, SAM-operators, artillerists and tankers. As of 1979, they had still not delivered even half of the equipment ordered two years earlier and were at least as slow in organising conversion courses for Syrian personnel. This was the reason why the SyAAF lacked modern interceptors to counter the IDF/AF, while the Syrian troops deployed with the ADF in Lebanon were still equipped with weaponry most of which had been proven obsolete during the October 1973 war with Israel.[5]

HUNTING PHANTOMS[6]

The difference between old weapons systems in service in Syria during the October 1973 Arab–Israeli War and those that were delivered after that conflict, became painfully obvious during the first new encounter between the IDF/AF and the SyAAF

A pair of F-15As from No. 133 Squadron, IDF/AF, in flight over Jerusalem, shortly after their arrival in Israel in 1976. (IDF)

A group of pilots from No. 99 Squadron, SyAAF, during an interview for the local press. Visible in the background is an R-3S missile installed on the launch rail under the centre of a MiG-23MS: the weapon was already hopelessly outdated in 1973 and would cost Syrian pilots several near-certain aerial victories in clashes between 1978 and 1981. (Albert Grandolini Collection)

since 1974. On 24 June 1979, a pair of Israeli RF-4E Phantom II reconnaissance fighters were detected by early warning radars of the Syrian Arab Air Defence Force (SyAADF) while approaching Beirut at high speed and altitude. Two MiG-21MFs – a version that entered service in the USSR in 1970 and in Syria in 1973 – were scrambled from the newly constructed Dhabba AB, outside al-Qusayr, but proved unable to intercept. However, a pair of MiG-23MSs from No. 99 Squadron, based at Dmeyr AB, were much more successful.

After passing high above Beirut, the two reconnaissance Phantoms turned north-west, then east, before turning round for the flight back home along the border with Syria. That was when the pair of MiG-23MSs caught up with them. Upon orders from their ground control, both MiG pilots – Major Abdul Rahman Hijazi and Captain Hayan al-Masry – engaged their afterburners and accelerated to Mach 1.5. Eventually, Hijazi came close enough to one of the RF-4Es to attempt an attack with R-3S (ASCC/NATO-codename 'AA-2 Atoll') infra-red homing, short-range air-to-air missiles. However, much to the dismay of the Syrian

EAGLES VERSUS MiGs: TAKE 1

With aircraft moving in three dimensions and very high speeds, no two crews – often not even the crew of the same aircraft – see the same engagement in the same way; even less so pilots from two sides at war with each other and flying entirely different aircraft. From what can be assessed from interviews with the Syrians who were involved and from Russian-language publications, the eight Syrian pilots involved in aerial combat with F-15s on 27 June 1979 were highly confident. Their MiG-21MFs were among the first in Syria to be rewired for two new types of infra-red homing, short-range air-to-air missiles – the R-13M (ASCC/NATO-codename 'AA-2C Advanced Atoll') and two R-60M/MKs (ASCC/NATO-codename 'AA-8 Aphid') – which the Soviet advisors claimed would outmatch anything in Israeli service. Moreover, most pilots had already encountered F-4Es and their AIM-7E missiles in combat and knew to counter these with shallow turns – about 20–30 degrees – to one or the other side. The Syrians thus planned to 'burn through' the opening volley of Israeli AIM-7s and engage the big F-15s in close-in aerial combat, where they expected the agility of their venerable MiG-21s, enhanced by the supposed superiority of their new weapons, would provide them with an advantage. According to the Israelis, six incoming MiGs were detected by the extensive network of communication intelligence (COMINT) and signals intelligence (SIGINT) stations that Israel had constructed in the north of their country, along the borders with Lebanon and Syria, and then tracked by early warning radar systems while approaching the Lebanese border. At that point, two formations of IDF/AF interceptors were directed to intercept them. A high-flying formation included four F-15s, while a low-flying group comprised two F-15s and two Kfir C.2s. Moments later, the Israelis activated their electronic countermeasures, completely interrupting radio communications between the Syrian pilots and their ground control. This is as far as accounts from both sides agree (except in regards of how many MiG-21s were around), there being at least two entirely different versions about what happened thereafter.[8]

According to the Israelis, the high-flying F-15 formation engaged first. Notably, no accounts by its leader, Benjamin Zinker, were published, and it seems he never opened fire or played any role in this combat – which is extremely unusual. As the range decreased to about 10 miles (16km), the other three formation members fired one AIM-7F each. The Israelis stress that all three Sparrows missed. Realising they were engaging interceptors, the first Syrian formation then attempted to disengage with a turn towards the north. While approaching a pair of MiG-21s crossing from his right to his left, the Israeli No. 2, Moshe Melnik, then fired one Python-3 from an unknown range and the missile scored a direct hit. Israeli No. 4 Joel Feldschuh then sighted the 'remaining' aircraft – i.e. what the Israelis thought was a second MiG – and fired another AIM-7F. Convinced that this would miss, Feldschuh switched to 'heat' and fired an AIM-9G Sidewinder shortly after. However, the Sparrow tracked correctly and scored a direct hit, followed by the Sidewinder that went for the fireball.

The second Israeli formation was about to engage the rear Syrian quartet head-on when Eitan Ben-Eliyahu, No. 3 of the high-flying IDF/AF formation, pounced upon it from above and the first two MiGs reacted with a steep climb. Ben-Eliyahu's AIM-7F missed its target, but the Syrians exposed themselves to the No. 1 of the second Israeli formation, Yoram Peled, who shot down a MiG-21 with a single AIM-9G missile. Ben-Eliyahu then turned back and attacked the second MiG and, because he was too close for missiles, shot it down using his M61A1 Vulcan cannon. Finally, with the Syrian formation completely broken, one of the MiGs fleeing eastwards was caught by two Kfirs and shot down by Captain Shai Eshel from No. 101 Squadron, using a single Python-3.

However, according to the Syrians, the Israelis opened the engagement by firing several Sparrows from about 20km. Because the motors of the AIM-7Fs released long white trails of smoke, the MiG pilots saw the missiles approaching them, but their usual shallow turns proved insufficient to evade them. Two AIM-7Fs hit home, killing one Syrian and forcing another pilot, one after the other, all four of his weapons failed to fire. The two RF-4Es thus continued southward unmolested, while the frustrated Syrians returned to Dmeyr AB to inspect their missiles and complain to their Soviet advisors.[7]

The obsolescence and vulnerability of the MiG-21 in comparison to latest US-made fighter jets and air-to-air missiles was to become even more obvious only three days later. Around noon on 27 June, several formations of Israeli fighter-bombers attacked three PLO bases between Sidon and Damour – striking further north than ever before. As usual, as soon as the Israeli aircraft entered the airspace north of Tyre, the SyAAF ordered its interceptors into the air: eight MiG-21MFs climbed to an altitude of 5,000 metres, turned west and accelerated to Mach 1. East of Sidon, they clashed with six Israeli F-15 Eagles and two Kfirs and lost five jets and two pilots.

LIGHT CONTACT

For the top Syrian military aviation officers – such as the Chief-of-Staff, SyAAF, Lieutenant General Mamdouh Hamdi Abazza (a veteran MiG-21 pilot) and the head of the Armament Commission and former Chief-of-Staff, SyAAF, Major General Mohammad Assad Moukiiad (a veteran Gloster Meteor pilot) – the loss of five old MiG-21s came as no surprise. Although not in possession of definite knowledge about the superiority of the F-15, they had been complaining to Soviet civilian and military representatives for years and demanding deliveries of advanced aircraft. What was surprising was just how superior both the F-15s and their new weapons were even to what the Soviets claimed was their 'best', such as the R-13M and R-60M/MK air-to-air missiles. Knowing they had no other options – because the Western powers had turned down all their queries about possible aircraft acquisitions there – the Syrians relaunched their efforts to get better aircraft from the USSR. Lieutenant General Tlass travelled to Moscow to demand deliveries of additional MiG-25s and MiG-27s, arguing that these could help establish balance with the Israeli F-15s. However, both the advisors in Syria and the government in Moscow turned down all related requests, and even the deliveries of MiG-25s ordered in 1978 continued at a very slow pace. SyAAF pilots thus had to keep

to eject from his stricken machine. Undeterred, the other six pilots pressed their attack home – only to experience the next big surprise: their opponents were F-15s and, although big and thus easy to see even through the severely constrained cockpit transparency of their MiG-21MFs, their high-speed manoeuvrability proved vastly superior to the old Soviet-made jets. As the first two formations merged, one of the Syrians broke hard to track an F-15 (perhaps Zinker) and managed to catch up with his opponent long enough to ripple-fire both of his R-60s. The Israeli accelerated away, causing both missiles to miss. However, the hard turn had slowed down the MiG so much that it then became an easy prey. It was subsequently hit somewhere in the rear and flipped out of control, forcing its pilot to eject. The rear formation of four MiGs attempted to catch the high-flying Israelis, when they were hit from below and their leader was shot down and killed. This blow and their shortage of fuel – caused by long ingress at Mach 1 – made it obvious that the battle was lost, and the remaining Syrians attempted to disengage in an easterly direction. Even then, another of the MiG-21MFs was hit: its pilot managed to nurse the badly damaged jet over Ryak AB before ejecting. The air battle thus ended with a clear-cut Israeli victory, with five 'kills' to zero.[9]

Starting in mid-1977, the entire fleet of Kfir C.2s (and Kfir C.1s upgraded to the same standard) was repainted in the same colours as the F-15s. This AIM-9G/H-armed example was photographed in flight low over the Dead Sea. (IDF)

Wreckage of one of five Syrian MiG-21s shot down by F-15s and Kfirs over Lebanon on 27 June 1979. Clearly visible is the roundel applied on the wing underside, between the two underwing hardpoints. (Albert Grandolini Collection)

EAGLES VERSUS MiGs: TAKE 2

For once, Israeli and Syrian accounts about air battles over Lebanon from 19 and 24 September 1979 were in agreement. In the first case, a pair of SyAAF MiG-23MS fighters were scrambled to intercept two high- and fast-flying RF-4Es over Lebanon. While the Israelis did not provide the reason for the failure of their opponents during the first engagement, the Syrians did. Both MiGs had been rewired for R-13Ms, and their pilots thus pressed home their attack enthusiastically. Indeed, both MiGs caught up with the Phantoms as they attempted to run away towards the south. The leader of the Syrian formation fired two missiles, his wingman one – both with the same result, the engines of their aircraft ceased working. The reason was that the R-13M's motor developed too much smoke, and when this entered the intakes upon the missile's launch, the engine surged. Both pilots found themselves busy relighting their engines, while their missiles failed to reach either target. From then onwards, MiG-23MS jets were usually armed with R-13Ms on underwing stations only, those under the fuselage remaining reserved for the R-3S.[11]

At least initially, the situation on 24 September was the same, with two RF-4Es entering Lebanese airspace at high altitude, and four MiG-21MFs being scrambled to intercept. However, contrary to five days earlier, this time the Israelis added a quartet of F-15 Eagles, which remained at low altitude, where no Syrian radars could detect them. As the Syrians crossed the border into Lebanese airspace at an altitude of 35,000ft (10,670 metres) and Mach 1, the Israeli ground control sent all four Eagles in to attack, and electronic countermeasures (ECM) were applied to interrupt enemy radio communications, causing the Syrian plan of action to fall apart. Piloted by Avner Naveh and Dadi Rosenthal, the first two F-15s fired one AIM-7F each from a range of about 10 miles. This caused the Syrians to split their formation, with one pair continuing straight ahead, intending to 'burn through' the Sparrows, and the other trying to outflank the Eagles. Naveh's Sparrow missed, but he promptly followed up with a Python-3, which blew up the leading Syrian MiG-21MF. Convinced his Sparrow was about to miss, Rosenthal also selected a Python-3 and fired: however, his AIM-7F then corrected its trajectory and proximity fusing while passing by its target, downing the second MiG just as its pilot was about to fire his R-13M into the Israeli jet. The second Syrian pair meanwhile turned around and attacked Rosenthal from behind, its leader firing his 23mm gun and claiming to have damaged the opponent. At that moment, the F-15s' No. 3 – Israel Shafrir – attacked from behind and his AIM-9G detonated next to the MiG-21MF No. 3, causing it to lose its braking parachute. The Syrian went into a dive and fled towards the north-west. The fourth MiG was caught while trying to disengage, Naveh shooting it down using his 20mm cannon. The SyAAF thus lost four additional MiG-21s and two of their pilots.[12]

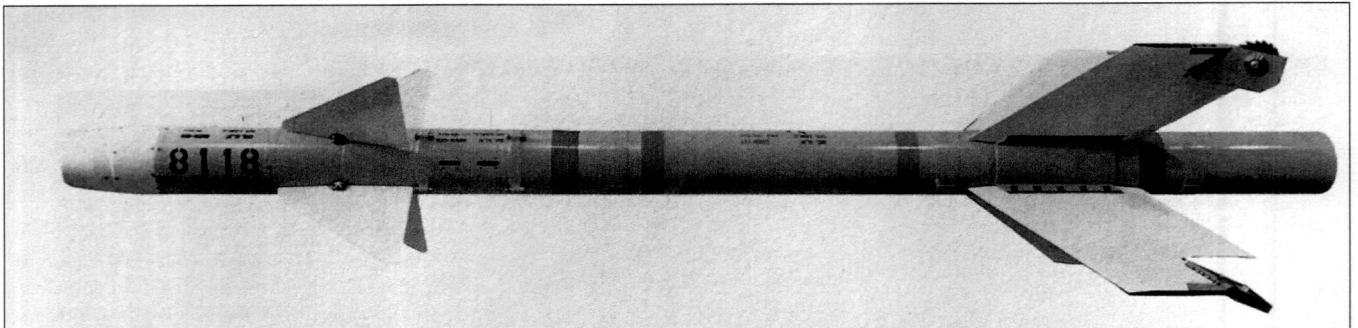

The Rafael Python-3 air-to-air missile, which quickly proved itself a deadly weapon during aerial combat over Lebanon in 1979. (Rafael)

on fighting with what was on hand – their Soviet advisors were constantly encouraging them to 'give it one more try'.[10]

To a certain degree, it can be said that the Israelis were playing into their hands because the IDF/AF continued flying both reconnaissance and air strikes over Lebanon for the rest of 1979. Thus, the Syrians were free to pick the time and place of the next aerial combat. However, the Syrians could not change the geography, which was to their disadvantage as the mountains of Lebanon blocked the view of their radars over the eastern Mediterranean Sea, from where most of the Israeli air strikes came. Unsurprisingly, neither anyone in the HQ of the SyAAF, in al-Mahdi Ibn Barakeh Avenue in Damascus, nor anyone in the SyAAF's interceptor units on bases around the country were under any illusions. Convinced they might have more success with one of the 'defenceless' Israeli RF-4Es, they launched another attempt on 19 September 1979, and failed for entirely unexpected reasons related to the Soviet bragging about the MiG-23MS and its R-3S missiles in aerial combat. When trying again only five days later, four MiG-21MFs were ambushed by escorting F-15s and cut to pieces by a combination of AIM-9Gs, Python-3s and gun fire. All four SyAAF jets were shot down.

INDIFFERENCE IN MOSCOW

Whether the Israelis had shot down eight or nine Syrian MiG-21s in aerial combat on 27 June and 24 September 1979, there was no denial that the SyAAF had suffered a very heavy loss, the F-15 having proven itself vastly superior to everything in service with the SyAAF. Syrian military aviation commanders had actually expected the superiority of the F-15, and had been warning the Soviets of this for some time. What did surprise them was the ease with which the Israelis not only jammed the SyAAF radio communications, but then also shot down so many MiGs. For Assad, Tlass and Chehabi, the loss of so many jets was a warning to stay away from the Israelis. Consequently, they devised the doctrine of 'light contact', under which, for the time being, their forces would avoid getting involved in larger battles and suffering additional losses. The heavy losses were the straw that broke the donkey's back, and in April 1979, Assad, Tlass, Chehabi, Moukiiad

Salah Attia in the cockpit of a MiG-21. Attia was the first SyAAF pilot to score a confirmed kill against an Israeli UAV, on 7 October 1979. (note that his helmet was painted dark red). (via R. S.)

and several other officers of the SyAAF and representatives of the Syrian economy all travelled to Moscow to demand urgent deliveries of modern aircraft. Once there, they explained to Brezhnev and other top officials about the heavy losses in aerial combat and the clear superiority of the F-15, adding that they could only expect additional encounters in the future to have similar outcomes. Much to their dismay, the Soviets treated them exactly as they had treated the Egyptians between 1970 and 1972, before President Sadat had ordered them out of the country. They received the fresh Syrian complaints with indifference. Indeed, not only the political leadership in the Kremlin, but the entire top of the Soviet General Staff remained in a ruthless denial of the advanced military technology the Syrians needed to compete with Israel. This denial would make them indirectly responsible for the deaths of all the Syrian pilots that the Israelis killed. Brezhnev and his aides quickly signed several pointless contacts relating to the provision of economic aid and promised to accelerate deliveries of the equipment ordered in 1977, but otherwise refused to accept any additional orders or provide more advanced aircraft.[13]

Ironically, it was during the Syrian delegation's visit to Moscow that the SyAAF achieved its only success of that year. On 7 October 1979, two MiG-21MFs from Dmeyr AB and one MiG-23MS from as-Seen AB were scrambled in reaction to an Israeli UAV that was detected over southern Lebanon, heading in the general direction of Dmeyr. One of the MiG-21 pilots, Salah Attia, finally sighted the UAV, managed to get in close and shot it down with a single R-13M.[14]

RENEWED INFILTRATION ATTEMPTS

Meanwhile, throughout May, June and July 1979, Israel was hit by a number of bombing attacks launched from within the Gaza Strip and the West Bank – both of which had been under Israeli military occupation, with massive pressure caused by illegal settlements, since 1967. No new infiltration attempts from Lebanon were undertaken by the Palestinians, however, and it remains unclear exactly what was on the Lebanese coast and why the fast missile boats INS *Atzmaut* and INS *Mishgav* targeted it on 17 July. During the following days, however, the commandos

of the 13th Flotilla are known to have ambushed several vehicles in the vicinity of Tyre. Indeed, measured by overall investment, very limited threat and meagre results, there remains much that is unclear about just what the Israelis were doing in Lebanon at the time. This is even more so considering that two years later, in the spring of 1981 during the election campaign in Israel, the Begin government released statistics regarding such attacks – these stated very clearly that of all the attacks aimed at Israel, only about 7.7 percent originated from Lebanon. The overwhelming majority – 92 percent – came from the Gaza Strip and the West Bank.[15]

The answer was that the PLO had renewed its infiltration attempts. Even if run on only a minimal scale, Begin saw them as confirmation of his doctrine. In the early hours of 17 August 1979, the Ras al-Bayada observation post detected a fast-moving vessel approaching Israel and directed a Dabur-class patrol boat to intercept it. An alert was sounded along the coastline from Rosh HaNikra to Mikhmoret, and fighter-bombers of the IDF/AF loaded with flare bombs were scrambled to illuminate the area. Eventually, a rubber boat with a crew of four was detected. Initially, the Palestinians managed to outpace the Israeli patrol boat, only to run into another one, whereupon the militants turned their vessel in a northerly direction and opened fire. Eventually, one of the Daburs managed to run down the boat, sinking it instantly. One of the militants was killed in the exchange of fire, but the three others were arrested. As far as is known, this was the first known case of the Palestinians actually trying to attack an Israeli warship.

Following a warning about two teams preparing an infiltration by sea, on 18 November 1979 the Rosh HaNikra surveillance post detected a fast-moving object approaching Israeli waters from the direction of Tyre. The information was promptly forwarded to the area control centre in Haifa, which swiftly ordered three Dabur-class patrol boats of the 914th Flotilla to intercept. An Israeli patrol boat underway near Tyre was too far away to intercept what turned out to be a Challenger boat powered by strong Yamaha engines. The second Dabur, in the Rosh HaNikra area, also failed to intercept. Concerned that this was a decoy, deployed in order to pull Israeli patrol vessels away from an actual attack, the Israeli command ordered its first vessel back to Tyre. Meanwhile, the boat near Rosh HaNikra reported that the crew of the Challenger speedboat was firing rockets towards the coast. Thereafter, the third Dabur-class boat – hull number 853, commanded by Lieutenant Osherov and originally patrolling the coast between Acre and Nahariya – was ordered to the scene. Osherov's crew detected the speedboat with the help of radar about 8km west of Achziv, switched on their searchlight and attacked with machine gun fire. The Palestinians fired back with assault rifles and an RPG-7, and several of their bullets found their mark, disabling the Israeli vessel's radar. Osherov ordered his crew to turn off the searchlight in order to avoid attracting fire and called for the Air Force and additional surface vessels to help. After about two hours, there was still no trace of the speedboat, and Osherov decided to search further away from the coast, believing the wind may have blown it in that direction. Eventually, the Palestinian vessel was found, half-burned and barely afloat, with its stern submerged and two of the crew hanging on to the side: two others had been killed in the earlier exchange of fire. Osherov managed to capture the two survivors and tow the badly damaged Challenger speedboat to Haifa.

As far as is known, this was the last Palestinian attempt to infiltrate Israel by sea until the early morning of 16 June 1980, when a Bertram-type boat was detected by one of the observation

WEAPONS CONFIGURATIONS

Israeli and Syrian interceptors that began clashing in Lebanese skies in June 1979 were armed with apparently similar weapons, yet actually of dramatically different quality. As delivered to the IDF/AF, F-15A/Bs were configured to carry four US-made AIM-7F Sparrow semi-active, medium-range air-to-air missiles and four AIM-9H infra-red-homing, short-range air-to-air missiles. According to the doctrine of the US Air Force, the Sparrow was actually the primary weapon of the Eagle, enabling it to engage from ranges out to 20 miles (32km). The AIM-7F was developed on the basis of experience from the Vietnam War, where Sparrows generally performed very poorly – primarily because of poor tactical training and lack of experience of US pilots, but also because the weapon was originally designed for intercepts of high-flying bombers, while over North Vietnam it was deployed against small and nimble MiGs, frequently at low altitudes. The AIM-9H, meanwhile, was the 'third generation' of the AIM-9D and AIM-9G Sidewinder – a version originally developed for the US Navy, whose fighter pilots preferred it to any other air-to-air missiles, and starting from 1968, received much better tactical training than their colleagues in the USAF. The AIM-9D entered service in Israel in 1970, followed by the AIM-9G in 1973. Both variants proved vastly superior to all other air-to-air missiles in service in the Middle East at that time. Indeed, thanks to their very wide engagement envelope, they enabled the IDF/AF Mirage III and F-4E Phantom pilots to score over 100 confirmed aerial victories against Algerian, Egyptian, Iraqi and Syrian MiGs during the October 1973 war, while suffering minimal losses in return. While AIM-9Gs and AIM-9Hs were reserved for use with F-15s, older AIM-9Ds were still deployed on Israeli F-4Es and Kfir C.2s in 1979, even if both aircraft were mainly used for ground attacks. Theoretically, the Phantom could carry up to four Sparrows and four Sidewinders (in addition to its internal 20mm gun), while Kfirs were usually armed with only two air-to-air missiles.

Starting in 1969, the Israelis introduced into service their first indigenous infra-red homing air-to-air missile: originally based on the poorly performing Shafrir-1 (or Shafrir Mk. I), the Shafrir-2 was not as sophisticated as the AIM-9D, but proved almost as effective, and – being credited with a total of 106 'kills' during its service life – greatly contributed to the IDF/AF establishing itself as the dominant air force in the Middle East of the 1970s. By 1978, the Rafael Armament Development Authority was in the process of introducing into service the third generation of indigenous air-to-air missiles: the outstanding Python-3. This extremely agile weapon was the first infra-red homing air-to-air missile in service with the IDF/AF with all-aspect capability – which meant that its nitrogen-cooled seeker head could track targets from the front and not only from

the rear. The Python-3s not only had a wider body diameter than the Sidewinders, but also wings of greater span, necessitating the use of adapters for installation on the F-15s. As of late 1979, it was already flight-tested and installed on both F-4Es (which never carried Shafrir-2s) and Kfir C.2s.

In comparison, as of early 1979, the primary air-to-air missile in the SyAAF arsenal was still the old Soviet-made R-3S. Originally developed on the basis of the US-made AIM-9B Sidewinder missile and entering service in 1961, this weapon belonged to the first generation of air-to-air missiles. It was designed for attacking high- and straight-flying targets, and had a very narrow engagement envelope. In Syria, the R-3S entered service with deliveries of the first MiG-21F-13s in 1963. Experiences from the June 1967 and October 1973 Arab–Israeli Wars had shown that entire batches of R-3S missiles were of very poor manufacturing quality, as not only did their seeker-heads easily overheat during high-speed operations, but at least a handful of cases are known where all four missiles carried by MiG-21s failed to fire. Moreover, even when scoring a hit, its small warhead rarely destroyed a Mirage IIICJ, never mind a jet as big and powerful as an F-4E.

Like so often before, the Soviets took a very long time to accept Syrian complaints about the missiles, and it was only once they agreed to deliver the MiG-21bis in 1978 that these arrived together with R-13Ms. Based on the AIM-9D, this had similar, not better performance and was slightly inferior in comparison to the AIM-9H. Even more was expected from an entirely new weapon: the small, light and agile R-60M/MK, delivered to Syria around the same time. Throughout 1979, the SyAAF worked hard to adapt both new weapons to its older interceptors, such as MiG-21M/MFs, MiG-21PFMs, MiG-21FLs and surviving MiG-21F-13s. Ultimately, the entire effort was in vain, for not only had the Israelis meanwhile brought much superior aircraft and weapons into service, but pilots flying the interceptors of the IDF/AF also enjoyed the advantage of being supported by a much better integrated air defence system and electronic countermeasures, which provided them with far superior situational awareness.

Top view of an F-4E armed with Python-3 air-to-air missiles. (IDF)

Almost all parties involved in the Lebanese Civil War used civilian utility vehicles as 'gun-trucks' or 'technicals' – with different weapons mounted on the flatbed. Shown on the left is a Land Rover Series II of the Tiger militia in East Beirut during the Hundred Days' War of 1978, while armed with an eight-pack of 2.7-in. SNEB unguided rockets (taken from the stocks of the FAL) and wearing clear identification markings to avoid 'blue-on-blue' incidents. On the right is a Land Rover operated by the pro-Syrian PFLP-GC, armed with a 106mm recoilless rifle. Both vehicles were originally painted in green overall, but the latter then received a camouflage pattern in desert yellow, which was common for Palestinian militias. (Artwork by David Bocquelet)

T17E Staghound armoured cars were in service with the Lebanese Army and Police from the late 1940s and proved highly popular – as they also did with various militias in the 1980s. This example, operated by the al-Mourabitoun, was armed with the British Ordnance QF 75mm gun, though the majority of the Lebanese Staghounds had either the original US-made M6 37mm gun or British Ordnance QF 2-pdr gun instead. As was common with the al-Mourabitoun, its original colour in light blue or grey blue was left as it was, indicating it probably used to serve with the Police (vehicles of the Lebanese Army were painted in light green or pale stone overall): atop of this, it has been marked with gaudy flags and slogans, using black, white and red – the colours of that militia. (Artwork by David Bocquelet)

The M42 Duster was the primary SPAAG of the Lebanese Army. Armed with the M2A1 twin-barrel 40mm gun, it was an almost perfect weapon for urban warfare. Due to its popularity, it was subsequently adopted by many of the militias, including the Phalangists, Tigers and the Arab Liberation Army, and saw combat in Tel Za'atar, the Second Battle of Faiyadiyeh and the Hundred Days' War. Originally, Lebanese Army Dusters were painted in light grey overall and wore the national insignia on their registration plates, but this colour was usually badly worn out – sometimes into light grey, like here – by the late 1970s. Different militias tended to apply their own insignia around the hull or on the turret. (Artwork by David Bocquelet)

Artillery was the strongest branch of the major Christian militias – both in north and south Lebanon – and especially once these began receiving Israeli support. Among the pieces provided from surplus IDF stocks were French-made Obusier modele 1950 (colloquially 'M50') 155mm towed howitzers, one of which is shown here, painted in blue-grey overall, with the muzzle in black – as operated by the Phalange and then the Lebanese Forces (also during the Battle of Zahle) in 1980 and 1981. In south Lebanon, Major Haddad's SLA deployed the M50s painted in the same fashion. The Israelis supplied ammunition and – very frequently – fire-control for the Christian artillery, often with devastating effect. (Artwork by David Bocquelet)

The nominally Christian forces in southern Lebanon started to receive US-made M3 halftracks from surplus IDF stocks in 1976 and 1977, and several dozen of them formed the backbone of Major Haddad's armour by 1979–81. They were usually left in their original sand grey overall colour, sometimes 'enhanced' through the addition of emblems for easier identification. This particular vehicle bears the insignia of the Kataeb Regulatory Forces and markings applied in celebration of 18 April 1979 – Lebanese Independence Day – when Haddad announced the establishment of the so-called state of Free Lebanon. The registration number remained in the same format as that of the IDF but lacked the letter 'צ'. (Artwork by David Bocquelet)

This BTR-152 APC (of Soviet design and manufacture) was probably captured from one of the Palestinian militias and operated by the al-Qulaia (or Qlaya'a) Battalion of the Guardians of the Cedars militia, led by Étienne Saqr. This militia originally started its days as al-Quat al-Lubnania, i.e. a unified body of all right-wing Christian militias, but later became an independent body – until 'integrated' into the Lebanese Forces by Gemayel's coup of 1980. This particular vehicle had been operated in the Christian enclave in south Lebanon, alongside Major Hadad's forces, and was also seen near the Israeli border. It was left in its original dark green overall colour but received various slogans and emblems over time. (Artwork by David Bocquelet)

The Lebanese Army acquired Alvis Saladin armoured cars in the 1960s, and they formed the armoured fist of its mechanised infantry components. By the late 1970s, around 200 were still operational with different factions. During the Syrian withdrawal of 1980, the reorganised Lebanese Army deployed Saladins and Staghounds to conduct road control and run patrols. A few were also sighted in service in southern Lebanon around the same time. All were painted in one-tone light grey overall, but this was badly worn out, while a few carried small Lebanese flags on their sides. (Artwork by David Bocquelet)

The UNIFIL contingents from France and Ireland both deployed French-made AML-90 armoured cars, primarily because of their excellent anti-tank capability. Although originally used as a 'show-of-force tool', the AML-90s of the IRISHBATT then saw combat during the fighting with Major Haddad's forces at At Tiri in 1980. As usual for all UN vehicles, they were painted in white overall, with large 'UN' letters in black on all four sides. The 'Irish touch' included the addition of the clover emblem on the side doors and the bow (the FREBATT usually applied the French roundel on the sides of the turret): the size of the emblem could vary. (Artwork by David Bocquelet)

The 44th Mechanised Infantry Battalion of the Royal Netherlands Army (44 PAINFBATT) deployed to south Lebanon in 1979, and its 170 vehicles included 58 YP-408 APCs in a total of seven versions. Six of these were equipped as anti-tank variants, with US-made BGM-71 TOW ATGMs, eight towed 120mm mortars, while others were equipped with radars or served as personnel and cargo transports for casualty evacuation, or even as command vehicles. All were painted in the regular UNIFIL scheme, in white overall, and wore only their UNIFIL registration numbers (in range 43xx) and those of the Dutch Army (KN xx-xx). (Artwork by David Bocquelet)

The T-55 – usually from Czechoslovak-licence production – was the primary MBT of mechanised infantry units of the Syrian Arab Army's contingent deployed with the ADF in Lebanon. This is a reconstruction of one of the examples deployed by the 47th Mechanised Infantry Brigade during the Battle of Zahle in the Beka'a Valley, where the type suffered heavy losses before it was properly protected by commandos of the 35th Special Forces Regiment. During the most intense period of fighting, the 47th lost about 20 T-55s, mostly to RPG-7s, but a few to Milan ATGMs too, and especially near the Bardouni Bridge. As was usually the case in the 1970s and 1980s, the tank was originally painted in dark green overall, on top of which the Syrians added a camouflage pattern in yellow sand and grey. The tactical insignia of the 47th Armoured Brigade (the colours of which remain unclear) and the registration were applied low on the glacis and near the top of the rear hull. (Artwork by David Bocquelet)

The T-62 remained the most powerful MBT in service with the Syrian Arab Army in the 1970s and 1980s, and was deployed exclusively by armoured brigades. Following their brief appearance during the fighting for Sidon in 1976, they appeared in the same area again in 1981, this time while operated by one of the units assigned to the ADF. This is a reconstruction of one from a company deployed during the Battle of Zahle in April 1981. By this time, the type still wore the regular camouflage pattern, on which the original dark green overall was partially overpainted by yellow sand, and partially with grey. Large turret numbers (522 in this case) were applied on nearly all the Syrian T-62s seen in Lebanon. (Artwork by David Bocquelet)

Syria acquired more than 350 Czechoslovak-manufactured VT-55 armoured recovery vehicles, based on the chassis of the T-55. They became known as 'BTS' in Syria and Lebanon, and at least four were assigned to the technical support service of every armoured or mechanised infantry brigade. This is a reconstruction of a BTS seen during the withdrawal of the Syrian contingent of the ADF from Beirut in February 1982. Note that while MBTs of the same unit wore the usual camouflage colours of dark green, yellow sand and grey, this vehicle received only a camouflage pattern in yellow sand atop of the original dark green. As far as is known, Syrian VT-55s wore no other insignia. (Artwork by David Bocquelet)

While in earlier times they used to be mounted on BMP-1 infantry fighting vehicles, by the late 1970s the primary mount of Syrian commando units became the BRDM-2. Although proving vulnerable to infantry-carried anti-tank weapons – such as RPG-2s and RPG-7s, as well as ATGMs – they still provided protection against bullets up to 12.7mm calibre. Large numbers of them were in service with both the 35th and 47th Special Forces Regiments, and one of them was destroyed by an RPG-7 in Zahle in December 1980, triggering a days-long intensive artillery bombardment of the city. On the positive side, BRDM-2s proved highly agile, capable of moving fast and turning even when at high speed, thus enabling the crew and passengers to survive many ambushes. This is a reconstruction of one of the BRDM-2s seen during the Battle of Zahle: as far as is known, it wore a camouflage pattern in dark green, yellow sand and grey, but no insignia at all. (Artwork by David Bocquelet)

By 1978-1981, the IDF/AF operated several types of UAVs, three of which saw most action. The AQM-34M-42L (main artwork), was deployed for high-speed high- and low-altitude photoreconnaissance with conventional cameras. Painted in white or light grey overall, the Tadiran Mastiff (lower left), was equipped with video cameras and used for artillery spotting. The most promising model turned out to be the IAI Scout (lower right), usually painted in sand and light earth on top surfaces and light grey on undersurfaces. Developed as a platform for 'beyond the horizon' battlefield reconnaissance, the Scout was a brand-new appearance in 1981, and became the first UAV to relay 'live' imagery of the Syrian SAM sites in the Beka'a Valley to the headquarters. (Artwork by Tom Cooper)

The first artillery battalion of the IDF to operate US-made M107 self-propelled howitzers was the 55th Drakon Battalion, which was directly subordinated to the Chief-of-Staff. Formed in late 1970, the unit became operational in March 1971 and was home-based near Refidim AB in Sinai. Its G Battery performed its first fire mission on 28 February 1972, and the entire battalion saw intensive involvement in the October 1973 Arab–Israeli War. Due to their excellent range, M107s saw heavy involvement in Lebanon. During the 1970s and early 1980s, all vehicles wore the IDF's UA902 sandgrey overall: tactical signs were regularly removed during operations close to the border or inside Lebanon. (Artwork by David Bocquelet)

French-made Aérospatiale SA.321Ks of the Israeli No. 114 '1st Heavy Lift Helicopters' Squadron saw heavy utilisation in relation to special operations into Lebanon during the 1970s. By the end of the decade, they were nearing the end of their service life, and were rarely deployed in support of paratroopers during raids between 1978 and 1981. However, they still – and frequently – operated inside Lebanese airspace, usually because they were flying 'VIPs' (commanding officers of the AMAN and the IDF) to visit Gemayel's headquarters in Jounieh and then returning them to Israel. As of 1978–79, they were still wearing a camouflage pattern in sand (FS33531), dark green (FS34227) and dark brown (FS30219) on top surfaces and sides, and light grey (FS35622) on undersides: by 1981, all the remaining examples were repainted in brown (FS30099) overall. (Artwork by Tom Cooper)

This is a reconstruction of one of the first batch of 11 Merkava Mk 1s issued to A Company of the 82nd Battalion, 7th Armoured Brigade, at the time this unit was formally declared operational during a ceremony at Sindiana firing range on the Golan Heights on 29 October 1979. The 7th Armoured Brigade completed its re-equipment with the Merkava in February 1982, when its 75th Battalion traded in its last Centurion/Sho't MBTs. All the Merkava Mk 1s were originally painted in UA902 sandgrey overall, and wore tactical insignia – even if without company emblems (these appeared only in 1982). Note the lack of loader's MAG machine gun. (Artwork by David Bocquelet)

The first M163 Vulcan Air Defence System self-propelled gun acquired by Israel became operational in 1974 with the 947th Golan Battalion (nicknamed the 'First Vulcan Battalion'). They were regularly deployed along the Lebanese border, and as well as air defence duties were often involved in ground operations. The M163 of the 947th Battalion with the registration 755319 צ, illustrated here, was credited with the downing of a Palestinian balloon on 16 April 1981. It was painted in UA902 sandgrey overall, and wore tactical insignia. Note that early M163s lacked large 'cages' applied on either side of the hull, while VADS turrets wore their own registrations because they were delivered separately from the vehicle. (Artwork by David Bocquelet)

From 1970, the IDF/Sea Corps started acquiring its first of an eventual 22 patrol boats from the US company Sewart Seacraft, powered by a 12-cylinder General Motors engine. Designated as Dabur-class vessels, these were equipped with Browning machine guns, Anschutz gyro, searchlight and Doppler radar. Twelve additional Daburs were constructed by the IAI Ramta plant and designated the Ben-Ami-class. All served with security flotillas, including the 914th (northern Mediterranean coast), 915th (Red Sea) and 916th (southern Mediterranean coast). By the late 1970s, they were undergoing upgrades, including the installation of a more powerful GM 16V92 engine, to better counter infiltrations from Lebanon. All were painted in the regular IDF/Sea Corps overall grey colour, with small, non-consecutive hull numbers in the range 85x to 89x for US-built vessels, and 901–912 for Israeli-built versions. Inserted is the service badge for the Dabur-class boats. (Artwork by David Bocquelet)

During the 1970s, the IAI Ramta plant developed a more powerful version of the Dabur, including the latest technologies, resulting in the Dvora-class fast patrol boat – one of the quickest and most-effective vessels of its class anywhere. Dvoras had a maximum speed of 37 knots and the capability to carry anti-ship missiles, even if the latter were rarely added. However, the project was rejected by the IDF/Sea Corps in 1978, probably due to the lack of funds, and the first four were sold abroad, while two were provided to Bashir Gemayel in a low-profile deal, along with two Yitush-class boats. All four were later returned to Israel, where the IDF/Sea Corps received its first Dvoras only in 1989. The vessels provided to the Lebanese Forces retained their grey overall livery, and only sported Phalange Party flags. (Artwork by David Bocquelet)

סופרקיק

672

As of 1979-1980, Israeli F-15A/B Eagles still wore relatively few markings atop of their standardised camouflage pattern in light ghost grey (FS36375) and dark ghost grey (FS36320) apart from the insignia of No. 133 'Double Tail' Squadron and their three-digit serial on the fin. Most of the time, their weapon configuration was quite standard for contemporary F-15s, and included four AIM-7F Sparrows in bays along the lower edge of intakes, and four AIM-9G or AIM-9H Sidewinders on underwing pylons. While flown by Yoram Peled, the jet with serial number 672 shot down a MiG-21 on 27 June 1979; on 13 February 1981, it shot down a MiG-25 while piloted by Benjamin Zinker. Around the same time, it received the nickname 'Tornado' in Hebrew, applied on the left side of the radome – a practice introduced to the entire F-15 fleet of the IDF/AF during that year. This F-15A was lost in a collision with F-15A '672/Vampire', on 15 August 1988, together with both pilots. (Artwork by Tom Cooper)

חץ-מקשת

704

Initially, No. 133 Squadron flew its first two-seat F-15Bs (serials 704 and 708) in combat as single seaters; the first qualified weapons systems officers joined the unit only in 1981. The F-15B serial number 704 scored the second-ever kill for the type, while flown by Joel Feldschuh, in air combat with Syrian MiG-21MFs, on 29 June 1979 – with an AIM-7F. In 1981, this jet received the nickname 'Like an Arrow from a Bow' in Hebrew on the left side of the radome. On 11 June 1982, Saul Simon and Amir Chodorov then claimed another Syrian MiG-21 while flying '704' resulting in the addition of the second kill marking. Depending on the task (top cover/combat air patrol or intercept), Israeli F-15s carried either one drop tank under the centreline, or a total of three drop tanks, including the one under the centreline and one under each underwing pylon: these are not shown for reasons of clarity. (Artwork by Tom Cooper

כוכב

695

The F-15A serial number 695 was one of the first modified to carry Python-3 air-to-air missiles. The large wings of that weapon necessitated their greater separation from the aircraft – initially in form of an adapter attached to the bottom of the underwing pylon. Because that installation prevented the carriage of drop tanks, better adapters, shown here, were developed by 1981. F-15A serial number 695 meanwhile became the most successful of the early Israeli F-15s, clocking two confirmed victories against MiG-21s while flown by Avner Naveh on 24 September 1979, and another against MiG-21 while flown by Yoav Stern on 31 December 1980 – two of these by Python-3s, and one by gun. In 1981, this jet received the nickname 'Star' applied in Hebrew on the left side of the radome. (Artwork by Tom Cooper)

Tom Cooper

This is a reconstruction of the Kfir C.2, serial number 874, flown by Shai Eshel on 29 June 1979, when he shot down a Syrian MiG-21MF with one Python-3 missile, thus scoring the sole aerial victory ever for the Israeli-made fighter-bomber. As had been standard since mid-1978, Eshel's jet was painted in light compass (or 'ghost') grey (FS36375) with a disruptive pattern of dark ghost grey (FS36320) on upper surfaces. No. 101 Squadron's insignia was applied on the upper centre of the fin, with that unit's traditional red and white stripes on the rudder. (Artwork by Tom Cooper)

Tom Cooper

A reconstruction of the F-4E serial number 165, from No. 119 Squadron, flown by Ran Granot and Zvi Erlich during the aerial combat in which they shared a MiG-21 kill with an F-15 on 31 December 1980. By that time, this Phantom was equipped with leading edge slats on the wings and an in-flight refuelling probe to the right of the cockpit. It wore the standard camouflage pattern in sand (FS33531), green (FS34227) and tan (FS30219) on upper surfaces and sides, and light blue (FS35622) on the undersides. The aircraft is shown as often deployed for a ground attack sortie, armed with two US-made M117 bombs on a triple-ejector-rack under each of the inboard underwing pods, and five M117s on the multiple-ejector-rack under the centreline. Adapters for Python-3 missiles were installed on the outsides of the inboard underwing pylons only. (Artwork by Tom Cooper)

Tom Cooper

The F-16A serial number 112 (US FY-serial 78-0314) was flown by Rafi Berkovich to score the first-ever aerial victory for this type: a Syrian Mi-8 shot down by 20mm gunfire on 28 April 1981. The jet is shown in configuration similar to the one during that mission, including four AIM-9Ls but with underwing drop tanks in addition to the centreline drop tank (additionally, it was loaded with 500 rounds of gun ammunition). Like all the 75 F-16A/Bs delivered to Israel from 1979–81, it wore a standardised camouflage pattern in sand (FS33531), tan (FS30219) and light green (FS34424) on upper surfaces, and grey (FS36375) on lower surfaces.

The three F-4E(S) that came into being as a result of Project Peace Jack in the mid-1970s, continued serving with of No. 119 Squadron, IDF/AF, through 1978-1981. Two of them had a fake 'black radome' painted on the nose: this example has its nose painted in radome tan. They saw heavy utilisation for reconnaissance purposes over Lebanon during this period and their sophisticated HIAC-1 LOROP cameras, installed inside a stretched nose, also enabled them to 'look' deep inside Syria. Their high-altitude operations tended to expose them to easy detection by Syrian early warning radars: this made these jets perfect 'bait' for SyAAF MiGs – a fact that Israeli F-15 pilots were more than happy to exploit. Notably, with high speed serving as their best protection, F-4E(S) usually operated without any underwing stores: even inboard underwing pylons were removed. Only when operating deep over Syria – and sometimes over Iraq – would they carry a single air-to-air missile on a special adapter installed in the front right Sparrow well. (Artwork by Tom Cooper)

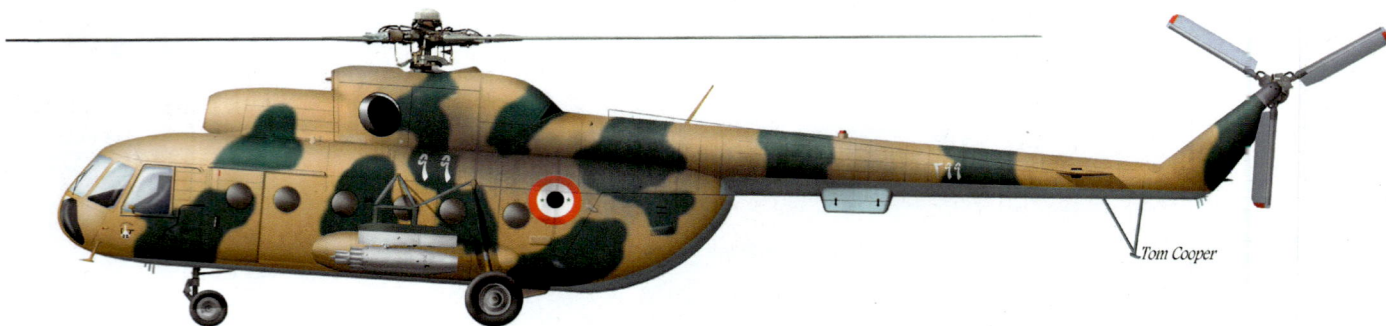

By 1978-1971, the SyAAF was operating a large fleet of up to 90 Mil Mi-8s: these were organised into two brigades (each with three squadrons of 12 helicopters) – one based at Marj as-Sultan AB, in south-eastern Damascus, the other at Taftanaz AB, in Idlib Province. All were originally delivered in dark olive green applied before delivery: initially, the Syrians would add a camouflage pattern in sand or orange sand atop of that. As the individual helicopters were sent for overhauls to 'The Works' – the SyAAF's central overhaul facility at Nayrab AB (the military side of Aleppo International) – they received a fresh camouflage pattern in orange sand and blue-green, as shown here. This example survived all the fighting of the 1980s and 1990s, but was badly damaged and abandoned at Taftanaz AB during the Syrian Civil War of 2013. Notably, SyAAF Mi-8s were regularly armed, usually with a pair of UB-16-57 pods for 57mm S-5K unguided rockets. This was the primary weapon with which they flew strikes on Phalangists in the Zahle area of 1981. (Artwork by Tom Cooper)

About 50 MiG-21MFs – and a miscellany of older variants of this prolific interceptor family – still formed the backbone of the SyAAF interceptor fleet as of 1979–1981. Most were delivered to Syria in 1973: a few before, but most during and after the October War with Israel. As of 1979, the majority of them still wore the original camouflage pattern applied before delivery, consisting of beige (BS81C/388) and olive drab (BS381C/298) – applied, 'more or less' to a standardised pattern – on upper surfaces and sides, and light admiralty grey (BS381C/697) on undersurfaces. As traditional since 1961, no national markings were worn on the fuselage: oversized roundels were applied on both of upper and lower wing surfaces, and fin flashes on either side of the fin. Notably, the fin flash in use as of 1979 was still the one of the Federation of Arab Republics – a lose union of Egypt, Libya, and Syria, 1972-1979 – and including the Hawk of Quraish (the tribe of Mohammad). Standard armament consisted of the GSh-23 cannon installed internally, and four R-3S air-to-air missiles. (Artwork by Tom Cooper)

Following a failure of negotiations for a union with Iraq, in 1980 Syria re-introduced the flag from the times of the United Arab Republic, including the tricolour in red, white, and black, and two green stars. This was also the national insignia applied on Syrian MiG-21bis. The first batch of 20 was ordered in 1977, but delivered only in 1979-1980, and thus most received only the new national insignia. All still wore the standardised camouflage pattern applied before delivery, in light stone (BS381C/361) and olive drab (BS381C/298) on upper surfaces and sides, and light admiralty grey (BS381C/697), on undersurfaces. Serials consisted of four digits in the range 2201-2299, and were applied in black on the forward fuselage, and below the dielectric fin-top. The new variant was armed with two new types of air-to-air missiles: R-13M (shown here on the inboard underwing pylon) and R-60M or R-60MK (outboard pylon). (Artwork by Tom Cooper)

After its troublesome service entry, the MiG-23MS remained a bitter disappointment for the SyAAF – even more so when jets of this type repeatedly failed to shoot down Israeli RF-4Es and F-4E(S)s underway over Lebanon in 1979-1980. The primary reason was that they were still armed with the near-useless R-3S air-to-air missiles, already obsolete in the late 1960s, and suffering from overheating of their seeker-heads when installed on MiG-23s. With the Soviets refusing to deliver anything better, the fleet of 16 original examples (serials 1600-1616) was only reinforced through attrition replacements (serials 1617 upwards). The entire Syrian MiG-23MS fleet wore the standardised camouflage pattern in beige (BS381C/388), dark brown (BS381C/411 or 450), and olive drab (BS381C/298) on upper surfaces and sides: the front portion of the undersurfaces was painted in light admiralty grey (BS381C/697), and the rear in medium grey (FS26162). Both MiG-23s and MiG-25s wore their national markings (including oversized roundels) in the same positions as the MiG-21s. (Artwork by Tom Cooper)

After demanding delivery of MiG-25s from Moscow for years, the Syrians were finally granted permission to order 28-30 such jets in 1977. Even then, the first MiG-25PDs arrived in Syria only in 1979. Expectations in Damascus were extremely high, because the combination of this type's top speed – about Mach 2.2 – and the 'long range' of R-40 air-to-air missiles – were praised as superior to anything in Israeli service. Unsurprisingly, MiG-25PDs were rushed into action almost as soon as the first unit operating them – apparently No. 5 Squadron – was declared operational in early 1981. All wore the standardised livery in camouflage grey (BS381C/626) overall: dielectric surfaces (radomes, antenna-covers etc.) were painted in dark gull grey (FS26311), while the lower surfaces and side of the engine nacelles were in 'neutral steel'. Their serials were in the range 2401 to at least 2430, and applied below the cockpit, and near the top of the fin. Insets show the primary weaponry of the type: R-40TD (infra-red homing variant) to the left, and the R-40RD (semi-active radar homing variant) to the right. (Artwork by Tom Cooper)

Southern Lebanon

Mediterranean Sea

BEIRUT

IAP

Khalde

Alei Muderej

Ain Dara

Ein Zehalta

Damour

Dayr Kamr Bayt ed-Din Barouch

Ba'aklin

Muktara

LEBANON

Jub Jenin

el-Bire

Sidon

Jezzine Masara Sukmur Kfar Kuq

Kfar Hune Dumr e'Beqa'a Rashia el-Wadi

LAKE KAROUN

AWALI

SHAMS

ZAHRANI

Eishiah

Nabatiyah Harat al-Hart

Hasbayya

Marjayoun

BEAUFORT CASTLE

LITANI

Khiyam

MT. HERMON

Tayybah Metulla Majdal Shams

Tyre Marrakah

Mas'adah

Rashidiyah

SYRIAN ARAB REPUBLIC

Houla Qiryat Shemona

Tibnin

Shaqra

Mays al-Jabal

UNDOF Zone

Yatar

Bint Jubayl Aytarun

Ayta ash-Shaab Ramot Naftali

Rosh HaNiqra Zarit Rmeich

Adamit Shetula Avivim

GOLAN HEIGHTS (occupied by Israel)

Nahariyya

Rihaniya

ISRAEL

HIGHWAY Zahle Shtura Musa

BEIRUT-DAMASCUS

LITANI

(Map by Tom Cooper)

The Palestinian speedboat knocked out by Dabur-class fast patrol boat 853 early on 18 November 1979. (Clandestine Immigration and Naval Museum, Haifa)

only ignored the challenge, but declared the massacre to be supported by Egypt, Israel and Iraq and an attack by Sunni extremists upon the Alawites, in turn hinting that the Brotherhood had similar intentions *vis-à-vis* all other minorities in the population. Immediately after the event, the government launched a country-wide campaign to uproot the Islamists. Within two weeks, about 6,000 were arrested, while 15 members of the Muslim Brotherhood imprisoned since 1977, and thus having no links to the massacre, were executed.

Arguably, the political leadership of the Brotherhood might not have known about the intentions of Yusuf and Uqla, but Uqla not only wrote the name of the Fighting Vanguard on a board in the mess hall where the massacre took place, but subsequently admitted the involvement of his group, adding that it acted independently from the political leadership. In reality, as of 1979, the Islamists controlled fewer than 10 percent of the insurgents that were active all over the country. Indeed, the armed resistance to Assad's rule of that time was no unified body, but consisted of numerous, loosely defined groups of various sizes, operating independently from each other. Indeed, as described above, even the Fighting Vanguard acted on its own. Thus, while few of the armed groups could have been described as affiliated with the Muslim Brotherhood, and some could be said to be better organised and equipped than others, actually they had no connection with the Islamists whatsoever. The secular opposition was actually far more numerous than the Islamist. However, to attract support from Alawites and other non-Sunni minorities at home, and backing from abroad, while tarnishing the reputation of the opposition, the government in Damascus branded all of the opposition as 'Islamists', and exclusively blamed the Muslim Brotherhood for the massacre.

As the security forces continued raiding and carrying out arrests around Aleppo, they sparked a number of street battles all over the city, which became fiercer the more the security forces reacted with repression. The violence in Aleppo literally exploded in November 1979 following the arrest of a regular leader of Friday prayers in the Great Mosque. Not only were there daily demonstrations, strikes and boycotts, but throughout December the militants attacked several offices of the ruling Ba'ath Party. In early 1980, the business district of the city – crucial for the economy of the entire country – was shut down by strikes and mass demonstrations. Before long, a similar situation began developing in Hama, Homs, Idlib, Dayr az-Zawr, Dera'a and Hasaka. By 8 March – the 17th anniversary of the coup that brought the Ba'ath Party to power – nearly all Syrian cities were paralysed by strikes, mass protests and even pitched battles between armed insurgents and security forces.[1]

posts near Nahariya. When the Dabur patrol boat 894, off Rosh HaNikra, attempted to intercept, it was hit by an RPG-7, which exploded in the kitchen, wounding two crew. The machine gunners of the Israeli vessel returned fire, hitting the speedboat and causing it to explode. All three Palestinians on board were killed.

5
'THE EVENTS'

Another irony of October 1979 was that it was during that month that Israel ceased flying air strikes against the PLO's bases in Lebanon – and it would not fly any further such strikes for more than a year after, irrespective of renewed infiltration attempts. Furthermore, Begin took this decision right at the start of a period when Syria under Hafez al-Assad was undergoing its most severe ever crisis. In 1980, the country was shaken by widespread popular unrest, large-scale protests and a continually intensifying insurgency. Thus, a strange situation developed in Lebanon where the IDF was launching one raid after another with ground forces against Palestinian bases, gradually expanding their size and scope, while the Syrians began withdrawing their forces from Beirut, although not actively involved in fighting Israel. Ironically, both thus acted to the benefit of Bashir Gemayel, enabling him to impose his hegemony over the majority of the Maronites and then not only plot actions aimed at forcing the ultimate Syrian withdrawal, but also at provoking an Israeli military intervention.

ALEPPO ARTILLERY SCHOOL MASSACRE
On 16 June 1979, Captain Ibrahim Yusuf, the officer on duty in the SyAA Artillery School in the Ramouseh district of Aleppo, in collaboration with Adnan Uqla and several other gunmen from the militant wing of the Muslim Brotherhood, the Fighting Vanguard (*at-Tali'a al-Muqatila*), machine-gunned a group of officers and cadets, killing 32 and wounding 54 others. The Brotherhood denied any knowledge of the carnage prior to its occurrence and that Yusuf and the group that committed the massacre were well-known to the Syrian authorities: indeed, they were active members of the Ba'ath Party. They challenged the government to provide evidence about any Islamist involvement. However, the government in Damascus – dominated by the Alawites – not

WITHDRAWAL OF THE ADF
Considering the spread of unrest at home, it is unsurprising that in January 1980, the Syrian contingent of the ADF was ordered into a

A column of Syrian Army trucks, loaded with infantry, withdrawing from Beirut in early 1980. (Albert Grandolini Collection)

any heavy armament, had only a minimal anti-armour capability and were operating mostly outdated equipment.

STANDOFF IN KIBBUTZ MISGAV AM

Independently from what was going on in Syria, during the night of 7/8 April 1980, a group of five members of the Iraqi-supported Arab Liberation Front cut through the border fence from Lebanon to Israel and reached the Kibbutz Misgav Am in Upper Galilee. After killing one man on the way, they took seven children and their night guard as hostages in part of their sleeping quarters. News of the attack

phased withdrawal from Beirut towards the east. Feeling insecure even in Damascus, Hafez al-Assad and his aides wanted to have their troops closer to home, and thus had them redeployed to the Beka'a Valley. This decision took the shaky Lebanese government of President Sarkis completely by surprise. Poorly informed about developments in Syria, they saw this decision as an attempt to destabilise Lebanon, perhaps even to drive attention away from the Soviet invasion of Afghanistan. They knew that the Lebanese Army was ill-prepared for such a sudden switch of power, and much too weak to replace the SyAA contingents that pulled out from key areas. However, Hafez al-Assad had other concerns and could not care less about Sarkis's problems. By the end of February, the ADF had withdrawn from Siddon, and then from East Beirut, retaining only a minimal presence in West Beirut and on key roads in the centre of the country. Meanwhile, re-equipped only with Staghound and Saladin armoured cars, a few AMX-13 light tanks and M113 APCs, the Lebanese armed forces promptly found themselves hopelessly outmatched: they lacked

reached the IDF Northern Command around 0100 hours, whereupon its commander, General Avigdor 'Yanush' Ben-Gal, assigned responsibility for the response to the 91st 'Galilee' Territorial Division.

The headquarters of the 91st Division deployed a fast-response team of seven members of the Golani Infantry Brigade's Reconnaissance Unit, who travelled to the kibbutz in two vehicles, reaching it around 0230 hours. As soon as the two cars passed the gates, the leading one, a Dodge D500, came under automatic fire that disabled the radio and punctured the tyres. Informed about the ambush, the commander of the 91st Division pressed for an assault, even though it soon became obvious that the unit was not ready: there was no intelligence on the number of opponents, no reconnaissance and the intervention team lacked suitable equipment. Nevertheless, the Golanis were ordered to close on the building and be ready to attack.

As the troops moved forward, they first ran into a fence that they had no idea about. While still working on getting through this obstacle, they received the order to launch their attack. Almost instantly, they came under heavy fire from assault rifles and were targeted by several hand-grenades. One of the Golanis was killed and three others wounded. Eventually, none other than the Chief-of-Staff, Eitan, ordered the team to withdraw and everyone involved to take time out to reinforce and make better preparations.

During the night, the kibbutz was secured by the police and elements from the 36th and 91st Divisions, including several teams of Unit 269 (better known as *Sayeret Matkal*, the long-

'Para recon': members of the reconnaissance unit of the 35th Parachute Brigade upon their return from a raid into Lebanon in 1979. (via The Paratroops Heritage Association)

range reconnaissance outfit of the IDF General Staff) and its commander, Colonel Uzi Dayan. Finally, Unit 7142 of the Service Dogs Unit (*Oketz*) and even Northern Command CO General Avigdor Ben-Gal appeared on the scene, together with the commander of the Golani Brigade Reconnaissance Unit, Colonel Giora Inbar. Together, they made comprehensive preparations, including eavesdropping on the building where the hostages were kept, and it was decided to operate in four assault teams: one from the Golani Brigade and three from *Sayeret Matkal*, supported by a back-up team and five sniper teams. Three of the assault teams were to be joined by the Service Dogs Unit. Multiple officers volunteered to join the attack, including Giora Inbar, who led the Golani team, Uzi Dayan, who led one of the *Matkal* teams, and his deputy Moshe 'Bogie' Ya'alon, who was left in charge of the forward command post.

Everyone was ready and in position for the assault when, at 0815 hours, the terrorists made contact to demand a helicopter that would take them and the hostages to Lebanon, with the Egyptian ambassador to guarantee such a deal. The Israelis acted as if in agreement with the demands, and at 1000 hours a helicopter appeared overhead, supposedly carrying the Egyptian ambassador. However, the helicopter was just a ploy to distract the attention of the hostage-takers away from what was happening on the ground. At 1015 hours, Ya'alon issued the command for the assault, and the teams went in. Within a matter of minutes, all five terrorists had been killed (two by Golanis and three by *Matkal* teams), and all but one of the hostages released: one child was killed in the crossfire, as was one service dog, while six members of *Sayeret Matkal* and one of the dogs were wounded.[2]

UNIFIL'S MINI-WAR FOR AT TIRI

The Israelis were not going to let the attack on Kibbutz Misgav Am go without a response. On the morning of 9 April, a task force of some 300–350 troops, 19 MBTs and 15 APCs crossed the border into Lebanon and the enclave controlled by Haddad's SLA, and drove by the positions of the Irish Battalion of the UNIFIL between Bint Jubayl and Adassieh, explaining to

the peacekeepers that they were on patrolling activity with the intention of preventing further infiltrations. Most of the task force was withdrawn back to Israel on 10 April and replaced by protected bulldozers and other engineering equipment, which relocated the border fence further into southern Lebanon and helped construct several additional outposts. In an attempt to distract UNIFIL from these activities, the Israelis then ordered Major Haddad into a provocation with the peacekeepers.

Commanded by Lieutenant Colonel Jack Kissane, the 46th Infantry Battalion of the Irish Army had arrived in Lebanon in November 1979 to replace the 45th Infantry Battalion (which had been part of the UNIFIL and headquartered in Naqoura since May that year). As was usual for situations of this kind, the unit assumed the official designation UNIFIL IRISHBATT, and proceeded to man numerous observation posts and checkpoints along the border – all of which were well-fortified to provide

An Israel-supplied M3 halftrack of the SLA in 1979 (see colour section for details). (Photo by Yosi Elmakis)

An AML-90 armoured car of the IRISHBATT at At Tiri in 1980. (UN)

Another view of an AML-90 of the UNIFIL IRISHBATT, in a firing position protected by stones and sandbags, on 1 May 1980. (UN)

maximum protection for their occupants. Additionally, mobile foot patrols were run both by day and by night. That said, the UNIFIL troops were rarely engaged by the parties involved in southern Lebanon and had thus so far suffered only minimal casualties and damage.

On 10 February 1980, during a visit to Manama in Bahrain, the Irish minister of foreign affairs made a statement in support of Palestinian rights. In the eyes of the IDF, this instantly converted the Irish peacekeepers into enemies of Israel, and three days later, on 13 February, Major Haddad's SLA began openly threatening them with retaliation. Over the following weeks, the SLA launched several minor attacks on the peacekeepers, but caused relatively little damage. The situation underwent a fundamental change in April, when Haddad decided to force the UNIFIL out of the outposts in At Tiri, a hamlet in the Bint Jubayl area, and Hill

880 above it, all manned by the Irish, along with troops from Fiji and the Netherlands.

Early on the morning of 10 April, UNIFIL observers reported a withdrawal of IDF vehicles in the direction of Saff al-Hawa and beyond. The movement continued throughout the day, and it appeared the Israelis were distancing themselves from the SLA. Then, at around 1300 hours, Haddad and 20 of his troops arrived at checkpoint 6-15A, held by the Irish, and demanded to enter At Tiri. The Irish turned him back, which initiated a tense standoff. Before leaving, Haddad shouted that his tanks would return and destroy the UNIFIL position. Indeed, just an hour after he had left, two SLA tanks and a few M3 halftracks climbed a hill about 1,000 metres further south, overlooking At Tiri. Haddad's troops later attempted to set light to Irish APCs at outpost 6-15D with a combination of flare and smoke grenades and sprayed them with small-arms fire. The situation quietened the next day, with only some minor exchanges of fire, but additional Lebanese tanks moved around the village and the peacekeepers.

At 1315 hours on 12 April, a group of about 50 civilians – mostly youngsters – arrived at checkpoint 6-15A and began plastering it and the Irish troops there with stones, bricks and bottles. When this had no effect, the group set several tyres on fire and rolled them down the slope towards the UNIFIL position. The peacekeepers spoiled this attempt to set ablaze their positions – or one of their

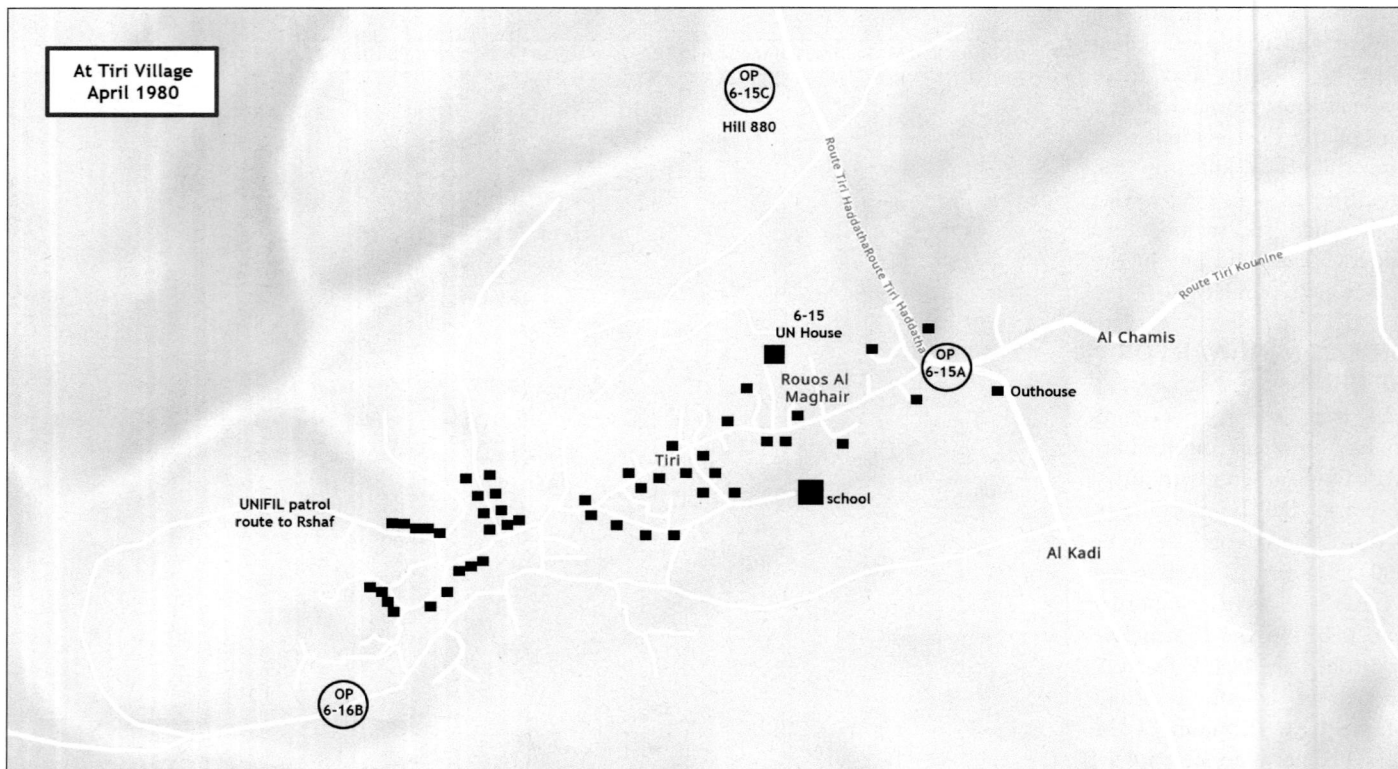

Map of At Tiri, showing UNIFIL's positions as of April 1980. (Map by Tom Cooper)

vehicles – but the civilians then attempted to enter the checkpoint en masse. Once again, the Irish stood their ground, forcing them away during the course of a physical confrontation and with help of tear gas. The SLA position near checkpoint 6-15 then opened fire at the peacekeepers, using the youngsters in between as human shields: the Irish responded with controlled fire, which grew in intensity as the civilians quickly withdrew.

At 1320 hours, the SLA intensified its fire, and began shelling both 6-15A and 6-15D. All the UNIFIL personnel took cover, but one Fijian solider was hit by a sniper and had to be evacuated to post 611 while under fire. Eventually, the Fijian peacekeeper succumbed to his wounds. UNIFIL now started to reinforce its fire, prompting the SLA to deploy one of its tanks, which fired three shells into At Tiri and then scored a direct hit on outpost 6-16. There were no casualties, but the explosion caused significant damage to the ground floor of the position. The Lebanese intensified their attack by spraying 6-15, 6-15A and 6-15D with heavy machine guns. Finally, the Dutch UNIFIL troops deployed on the nearby Hill 880 opened fire with their BGM-71 TOW anti-tank guided missiles, followed by other peacekeepers in At Tiri: a halftrack of the SLA was destroyed by a direct hit from an AML-90 of the Irish at around 1340 hours, and at least one of Haddad's soldiers was killed, with another suspected killed and three taken prisoner.

The exchanges of fire continued throughout the afternoon. Between 1543 and 1728 hours, the SLA fired several tank shells at checkpoint 6-15A, and also sporadically poured fire at 6-15 and 6-15D, as well as into At Tiri. This time, the UNIFIL troops on the hill east of 6-15A received permission to retaliate, and consequently opened fire. However, at around 2100 hours, Haddad suddenly launched an attack on outpost 6-24 and captured four peacekeepers. Nevertheless, this action brought the clash to an end: realising he could not force UNIFIL away from At Tiri, Haddad gave up and agreed to exchange all his prisoners. This was done the following morning, when he received the body of one of his troops and the wreckage of the destroyed M3 halftrack. The 46th Battalion of the Irish Army ended its tour of duty in Lebanon later the same month.

HIGH VOLTAGE[3]

The foray into southern Lebanon on 9 April 1980, and the SLA attack on the IRISHBATT at At Tiri two days later, caused a further uproar in the international community, creating sufficient pressure for Israel to announce a complete withdrawal 'after completing certain engineering tasks'. Nevertheless, UNIFIL observers reported about 145 Israeli troops, 12 MBTs and six APCs still present between the villages of Markaba and Chaqra on 11 April: these moved south of the border only three days later. For all practical purposes, the withdrawal was incomplete even then, for the IDF continued to operate inside Lebanon – but now in the form of small teams of special forces, foremost among them the Long-Range Reconnaissance Unit 869 and the Reserve Intelligence Unit.

Furthermore, the General Command of the IDF decided to deploy the commandos of the 13th Flotilla, IDF/Sea Corps, for a retaliation attack on the ALF's camp near Sarafand. Located in a small bay on the Mediterranean coast, with shallow waters, the site had been under surveillance for some time already. The intelligence gathered concluded that a team of the Arab Liberation Army was in final preparations for an infiltration attempt. Because the camp was approachable from the sea only, a decision was taken

Israeli paratroopers exiting the cargo hold of an S-65 helicopter following a raid into Lebanon during 1979. (IDF)

to raid it with combat divers. A mission plan – Operation High Voltage – was developed by 9 April, and the team was in position two days later, but the mission did not receive the green light from the Ministry of Defence (at the time, Menachem Begin acted as both prime minister and minister of defence). While waiting for approval, the Naval Command decided to continue preparations, including a final exercise on a model of the camp. It split the objective into three parts: a dug-in and concealed compartment nicknamed the 'rabbitry', a two-storey building believed to be housing the headquarters and a single-storey building serving as a living compartment with an ammunition bunker nearby. It was assessed that there were about 30 combatants present. The planers of the operation anticipated two complications: one was related to the fact that the bay was narrow and surrounded by a rocky shore, while the other was that all approaches to the three objectives on the coast were covered by dense vegetation and multiple irrigation and drainage ditches, making it hard to control the force and its synchronisation.

The raiding team was led by the commanding officer of the 13th Flotilla, Colonel Ami Ayalon, who distributed his 47 operators into five sub-teams: one forward-commanding team (including himself and a medical doctor), three teams to attack the three objectives and one recovery team waiting on rubber boats off the cost. The teams were taken to Lebanon with the help of four missile ships of the Naval Command, including INS *Yaffo* (a Sa'ar-4-class corvette, which served as the command post and carried the Chief-of-Staff, Eitan, and the commander of the 3rd Flotilla, Colonel Avraham Ben-Shoshan), INS *Ga'ash*, INS *Hanit* and INS *Hetz* (Sa'ar-3-class corvettes). As well as serving as troop transports, the four ships were tasked with running a deception operation and recovery of the raiding team. The recovery team included 11 Zodiac Mk 5 rubber boats and three Snunit fast attack boats, all commanded by Lieutenant Colonel Uzi Livnat. Finally, the IDF/AF assigned one of its Sikorsky S-65C-3 helicopters of No. 114 Squadron for search and rescue purposes and had a squadron of fighter-bombers on alert.[4]

The task force set out late in the afternoon of 17 April. Upon reaching a suitable jump-off point, the assault teams unloaded and embarked their Zodiacs: during the pre-mission testing, engines on three of the boats had malfunctioned, forcing commanders into the decision to leave the back-up team on INS *Yaffo*. Guided by the Snunit boats, the remaining eight Zodiacs then moved over the rough sea towards their objective. Around midnight, they reached a position about 2km short of the coast, and the divers dropped into the water. However, while approaching the coast, the teams realised that they have been dropped at the wrong position and

An S-65/CH-53D/Yas'ur helicopter during an exercise with a Dabur-class fast patrol boat in 1979. (via Ofer Bar-Shalom)

had to shift to their south-west. This caused a 40-minute delay in them reaching the coast. Once on the beach, they encountered another surprise, as the planned route to the target was full of dry leaves and dense grass, movement through which would cause too much noise. Ayalon thus decided to make an approach via a nearby ploughed field. Even then, the raiding team encountered yet more problems. Underway to the main objective, one of the attack teams ran into an irrigation construction that was more than 2 metres tall. At this point, Ayalon split the force into two. He let one team continue towards the one-storey building and the bunker in the south-east of the camp, while the other three turned back to approach via the dense grass full of leaves, regardless of the noise this would cause.

Around 0211 hours, all the teams were finally ready to launch the assault. Wasting no further time, Ayalon ordered them to attack. While rushing towards their objectives, the commandos sprayed the targets with small-arms fire, and then threw hand-grenades through windows and doors. A pickup truck parked nearby was destroyed by a rifle-grenade. During the attack on the two-storey building, a team member responsible for the explosive charges failed to open the rucksack containing them and was ordered to throw the pack with both of them into the building. The resulting detonation was so powerful that the building collapsed, and the team-leader was wounded by debris. The single-storey building was demolished in similar fashion, with the help of three explosive charges thrown through the windows, one after the other. Around that point, one of the Palestinians approached the command team thinking they were 'friendlies' (apparently, he was misled by one of the officers speaking fluent Arabic) and was shot dead. The third team experienced some problems with finding the entrance to the 'rabbitry' in the tall grass, but eventually reached and demolished it too.

At 0245 hours, Eitan gave the order to conclude the mission and evacuate. All the teams pulled back to gather on the shore further south than planned, because the surviving ALF members were meanwhile alerted and pouring machine gun fire in their wake. The commandos loaded the wounded and the doctor into an inflatable rubber boat and swam with them towards the pickup point. The warships waiting off the coast then opened fire, aiming to suppress the surviving ALF forces. All teams were back on the ships by 0440 hours, and the flotilla headed back to Israel. The sole S-65 helicopter was then called in to evacuate two wounded commandos.

The raid on the ALF camp near Sarafand was a huge success, especially considering the number of complications experienced by those involved in the operation. A post-mission de-brief assessed it as achieving complete surprise, destroying all three objectives and killing between 15 and 20 militants (apparently including the team that prepared the infiltration and resulting attack on Kibbutz Misgav Am), and this at a cost of only two wounded.

MAN OF BLOOD AND LEADER[5]

The Northern Command of the IDF was meanwhile developing plans for several additional raids. The first of these became a long-range, heliborne attack on the ALF base near the Qasmiyeh crossing, some 25km north of the Israeli border. Codenamed Man of Blood, this operation was very complex because of reports about the possible presence of multiple anti-aircraft pieces and the relative distance of the objective from friendly lines. The planning was closely supervised by the CO of Northern Command, General Ben-Gal, and preparations included the construction of a very precise model of the ALF stronghold at the IDF training base at Elyakim, on which a wide range of situations – including an evacuation by air and sea – were exercised. The unit assigned for the mission was the 35th Parachute Brigade (commanded by Colonel Doron Rubin), and officers and other ranks from nearly all of its elements – altogether 98 men – were to become involved, together with a Unit 5101 team, a back-up force of the Golani Infantry Brigade.

Operation Man of Blood – the first 'long-range' heliborne assault by the IDF into southern Lebanon – was launched on the night of 29/30 June 1980 and proceeded without any complications – primarily because the ALF offered much less resistance than expected. Eight Palestinian combatants were killed and one captured, while the IDF suffered no injuries.

The next plan that was realised, codenamed Operation Leader, was even more complex. This enterprise included the involvement of two task forces:

- Parachute Task Force: five company-sized combat teams from the 50th, 202nd and 890th Parachute Battalions, the Parachute Brigade Combat Team (commanded by Shaul Mofaz, and including elements from the 202nd and 890th Battalions and the Brigade Engineering Company) and the Reconnaissance Unit of the 35th Parachute Brigade, with a Forward Controllers Team (led by Doron Rubin).
- Golani Task Force: four combat teams from the 12th, 13th and 51st Infantry Battalions and the Reconnaissance Unit of the 1st Golani Infantry Brigade, with a Forward Controllers Team (led by Ilan Biran) and a team of Unit 269, commanded by Colonel Uzi Dayan.

Artillery support for both task forces was provided by the 282nd Artillery Brigade of the 36th Division, deployed in the Marjayoun area.

Both task forces moved at once, late in the evening of 18 August, from al-Qulayah and Marjayoun. After crossing the Litani River, the Golani Task Force advanced on Arnoun, while the Parachute Task Force moved in the direction of Nabatiyah but experienced delays caused by rough terrain. The hold-ups eventually resulted in the postponement of H-Hour. Because of the delay, the combat group of the 12th Golani Battalion was spotted by the Palestinians and came under fire, losing the element of surprise. Consequently, all units now had to act in a hurry, without any synchronisation. The Golani Task Force pushed for Arnoun under heavy fire from several fortified positions, losing an officer of the 51st Battalion and a member of the Reconnaissance Unit killed, and several wounded, some of whom had to be evacuated. The 282nd Artillery Brigade then joined in the battle, hammering Palestinian positions, but on the orders of the task force's headquarters, all artillery support ceased when a single S-65 helicopter arrived, which resulting in the troops finding themselves in trouble. Regrouping and then launching their assault, the Golanis managed to capture and clear Arnoun, demolishing multiple buildings and destroying several Fatah vehicles in the process.

With the Golani Task Force engaged in firefights with the Palestinians, the Parachute Task Force had no choice but to assault its objectives without any delay. The 890th Battalion ran into enemy fire while approaching Kfar Tebnit, and promptly lost the commander of its leading element killed and two other troops wounded. The rest of the team retreated until the battalion CO managed to restore order and personally lead a new attack that secured this objective. The other two battalions reached their targets without any complications, destroyed several buildings and a bunker and captured two Palestinian militants. Meanwhile, Shaul Mofaz led the Parachute Brigade Combat Team in an attack on Mazra'at Ali el-Tah, which appeared to be abandoned, but his troops then came under fire from the direction of the Golani Task Force's advance. Having accomplished their tasks, the paratroopers withdrew to the pickup point, all the time harassed by Palestinian artillery fire from Nabatiyah. Their evacuation was then performed by several S-65 helicopters.

Both task forces were back in Israel by 0600 hours on 19 August. Overall, they reported killing 60 Palestinians and taking two prisoners, demolishing 10 buildings and destroying several vehicles and artillery pieces. In turn, the IDF lost three men killed and 12 wounded during the operation.

BLOOM AND SIGAL

The next two Israeli raids into southern Lebanon were, in general, very similar – in terms of the involved units, the operational profile and tactics, and the area that they targeted. The primary differences were that both were undertaken proactively (i.e. not in retaliation for Palestinian attacks), and that a Navy Commando unit was deployed to assist in the crossing of the Litani River. Operation Bloom was launched late on 16 October 1980 from al-Qulayah and Marjayoun, over the Litani to the village of Jarmaq and the ALF base west of it. A combat team of the 12th Battalion of the 1st Golani Infantry Brigade cleared the village, while a joint force of paratroopers, reconnaissance and anti-tank units captured the stronghold from which artillery was deployed both against northern Israel and Christian enclaves further north. The blocking force – drawn from the 13th Battalion of the 1st Golani Infantry Brigade – engaged and destroyed two technicals. With all objectives accomplished, both task forces withdrew back over the Litani and were then picked up by S-65 helicopters, reporting between 10 and 15 militants killed, six buildings demolished and two vehicles knocked out – without suffering any casualties themselves.

Operation Sigal followed the same scheme but targeted the village of Mahmoudiyeh and involved paratroopers from the 202nd and 980th Battalions, with reconnaissance and engineering units of their brigade, and a task force from the 1st Golani Infantry Brigade, with its reconnaissance unit. The IDF is known to have suffered one killed and three wounded during this operation.

ALEPPO AFIRE[6]

By this point, the situation in Syria was on the brink of running out of control. Focusing upon Aleppo as the source of the uprising, Hafez al-Assad ordered the 3rd Armoured Division – commanded by Major General Ali Haydar – into the city. Nominally at least, this crack armoured formation – 15,000-strong and equipped with T-62 MBTs and BMP-1 IFVs (infantry fighting vehicles) – was staffed by carefully selected officers and other ranks, better paid and trained than the rest of the ground forces. It acted as the strategic reserve of the SyAA, and Damascus expected it to be more loyal and dependable than other elements of the army. However, contrary to Lebanon in 1976, in 1980 its opponents were not foreigners but Syrians, which is why Assad had second thoughts about the division's loyalty. Therefore, he reinforced it

INFILTRATIONS BY AIR: TAKE 1

If there was one Palestinian militant faction that demonstrated special creativity in planning infiltrations into Israel, it was the Palestinian Liberation Front – a faction of the PLO led by Muhammad Abu al-Abbas. The first indications that the PLF was preparing something special came in early 1980, when the AMAN received intelligence about Ahmad Jibril's PFLP-GC preparing a 'suicide mission over the air'. By June, Jibril made it public that his organisation had 'dozens of trained pilots … some capable of flying supersonic jets', and all were 'ready to fly bombing missions' – in essence infiltrating Israeli airspace, finding their targets and diving into them. Indeed, at that time numerous PLO cadets were undergoing pilot training – especially in Libya, and a few (with Libyan passports) even in

Yugoslavia. However, there was no indication of any of them being involved in preparing anything 'unconventional'.

On 20 July 1980, the Ghana Battalion of UNIFIL reported a 'fierce explosion' somewhere between Tignine and Majdal Selm. Several days later, a local shepherd found the wreckage of a large balloon on a hillside, which turned out to have been powered by two propane tanks intended for domestic use. Apparently, one of the tanks exploded, causing a fire that wrecked the gondola. UNIFIL soldiers inspected the area and found no trace of the crew, but several firearms and ammunition, about 20kg of plastic explosives with delay fuses and a detailed map of northern Israel. At that time there was no clue about the target and no details about the mission or the origin of the crew.

Wreckage of the balloon deployed by the PLF for its second aerial infiltration attempt on 17 April 1981. (IDF)

with a similar-sized contingent of the Defence Companies (*Saraya ad-Difa*, SAD), commanded by his brother, Rifa'at al-Assad.

After surrounding and sealing off Aleppo, the troops – supported by MBTs, IFVs and helicopters – drove down the main streets on 1 April to interrupt communications between individual districts, and to surround and separate them. Finally, they launched a house-to-house search for suspects and weapons. This operation went on for the rest of the month and resulted in hundreds of summary executions and thousands being detained inside a makeshift prison camp in the citadel of Aleppo. By early May, the government had re-established control of the city. Nevertheless, the situation remained tense into the summer, during which several military patrols were ambushed and a number of soldiers killed. Similar tactics were then applied by government forces in Hama and Dera'a a few weeks later, resulting in an unknown number of civilian casualties.

BASHIR'S COUP

Amid the growing chaos and tensions, on 23 February 1980, Bashir Gemayel narrowly evaded an assassination attempt: the bomb meant to blow him up killed his 20-month-old daughter, Maya, and other civilians in East Beirut, and wounded more than 30. On 12 March, another remotely controlled bomb went off in Dora, on Mount Lebanon, this time narrowly missing Chamoun but killing one of his bodyguards. Through late March and early April, tensions developed between the Iranian-supported

Amal and Fatah, which also resulted in numerous high-ranking assassinations. Furthermore, on 22 April, gunmen of Frangieh's Marada Brigade attacked a group of civilians in Shamout, killing up to 20 and abducting several others. Then in May, the ZLA attempted to drive the Phalange out of several villages in the Batroun area, on the coast, provoking a five-hour gun battle that left 20 dead.

It was at this point that the Israeli pressure on the Maronite militias to unite and form one regular force seems to have brought Bashir Gemayel over to the idea, and in his typical fashion, late on 7 July, he deployed the Phalange in a surprise attack on the headquarters of the Tiger militia of the NLP. The commander of the Tigers, Dany Chamoun, was preoccupied with his mistress at the time, and thus managed to escape the attack, fleeing to Europe. However, the brief yet savage attack left over 80 of his combatants dead. The Tiger militia all but collapsed over the following hours, with Phalangists quickly seizing its offices in Beirut, many outlying bases and large sectors of the front lines, together with most of its heavy weapons – including several Israeli-provided M50s. By the end of the following day, and at the price of more than 300 killed and over 500 wounded, Gemayel controlled East Beirut and the northern Christian enclave. Although being unable to overcome Frangieh's ZLA and the Armenian Dashnak in Bourj Hammond and Camp Marash, he quickly announced a merger of 'all the Maronite militias' into the Lebanese Forces (LF). Actually, not even all of Chamoun's own men joined the new organisation,

EAGLES VERSUS MiGs: TAKE 3

Throughout 1980, Damascus was preoccupied with events at home, and the SyAAF was thus held back in case it became necessary to fight the insurgency. However, complaints from the PLO eventually prompted Hafez al-Assad to order Abbaza's fliers into another intercept attempt. A suitable opportunity emerged on 31 December 1980 when the Israelis flew an air strike against Palestinian strongholds in the Nabatiyah area. With this town being less than 15km from the Syrian border, the SyAAF scrambled four brand-new MiG-21bis interceptors, all armed with the usual mix of two R-13M and two R-60M/MK missiles. However, no matter what the Syrian pilots tried, it was in vain, as the superior Israeli command, control and communication (C3) system detected them early and pairs of

F-15s from No. 133 'Twin Tail' Squadron and F-4E Phantom IIs from No. 119 'The Bat' Squadron were ordered to intercept. Realising the element of surprise was lost, the Syrian ground control turned its formation away, but the Israelis were faster. The Israeli No. 2, Yair Rachmilevic, destroyed one MiG-21 using a Python-3 missile. Meanwhile, his section leader, Yoav Stern, and the two Phantoms all went after another Syrian interceptor. The weapons system of the lead F-4E malfunctioned, but the wingman – crewed by Ran Granot and Zvi Erlich – latched on to the enemy jet and fired a single Python-3 around the same time that Stern launched an AIM-9G: both missiles scored direct hits, completely destroying the MiG-21bis and resulting in a 'shared' claim by the two IDF/AF crews.[9]

A view from the cockpit of one Israeli F-15A towards another. Notable is not only the highly effective 'ghost grey' camouflage pattern, but also the launch rails for AIM-9G/H/L Sidewinder air-to-air missiles installed on either side of the underwing hardpoints. (Government Press Office)

but the blow against the Tigers caused enough concerns for Étienne Saqr – leader of the Guardians of the Cedars – and various other leaders of smaller militias to announce they were joining the LF. Bashir Gemayel thus imposed himself as the leader of the majority of the Maronite community and, with Israeli support, moved to effect his ultimate design: spoiling the Syrian position in Lebanon and provoking an Israeli military intervention.[7]

EVENTS OF 1980

In Syria, Hafez al-Assad found little respite during that summer. On 26 June, the Muslim Brotherhood launched an assassination attempt against his convoy of cars in Damascus. The revenge for this was bloodier than ever: only a day later, an estimated 1,152 inmates of the notorious Palmyra prison were massacred by Rifa'at al-Assad's SAD, and even membership of the Islamist organisation was outlawed. When the insurgency continued nevertheless, Assad reverted to

his usual tactics from Lebanon. On 1 July, SAD troops randomly rounded up some 200 males in the Suq al-Ahad area of Aleppo and massacred at least 40. When the insurgents staged another ambush against the troops of the 3rd Armoured Division and killed several of them, on 11 August the SAD surrounded the al-Masharqah neighbourhood, detained several hundred males – including

A clandestinely taken photograph showing the headquarters building of the Soviet military assistance group in Damascus. (CIA)

A SyAA BRDM-2 armoured scout car on the streets of Zahle in late 1980. (via Efim Sandler)

Bashir Gemayel in a still from a video taken around the time of the Battle of Zahle. (via Albert Grandolini)

dozens of children – and summarily executed them. Eventually, in exchange for about 300 government officials, Ba'ath Party members and soldiers assassinated by insurgents, between 1,000 and 2,000 citizens of Aleppo were killed in 1980 alone, and up to 8,000 detained by the security forces. What subsequently became known as 'The Events' in Syria was now about to reach its peak.

As could have been expected, mindless brutality against uninvolved civilians only resulted in further radicalisation of the Muslim Brotherhood of Syria, and another escalation of the insurgency. Through the second half of 1980, the Islamists not only continued assassinating Ba'athists and military officers but began systematically attacking military bases housing Soviet instructors – either with small-arms fire or mortars. After several Soviet officers were killed, Moscow's chief military advisor in Syria, Lieutenant General B. Budakov, felt forced to order a withdrawal of all of his troops to one base in Damascus, where they could be suitably protected. It was only at that point that the Soviet government became sufficiently concerned about the future of Hafez al-Assad's government and – less than a year after launching a military intervention in Afghanistan – ordered an unprecedented step *vis-à-vis* Syria. In October 1980, Hafez al-Assad was invited to Moscow for urgent talks. As result, the Syrian Arab Republic and the Soviet Union signed a Treaty of Friendship and Cooperation that, among other terms, stipulated closer cooperation between their armed forces and a deployment of 4,000 additional Soviet 'advisors' in the country. For all practical purposes, the USSR thus launched a low-scale military intervention in Syria.[8]

6

BATTLE OF ZAHLE

Having consolidated his control over the majority of the Maronites, in mid-1980 Bashir Gemayel redirected his attention to damaging the Syrian position in Lebanon and inciting an intervention by the Israeli military.[1]

FROM GOAT TRAIL …

The most suitable objective for the young Maronite leader turned out to be Zahle. The third-largest city in Lebanon, positioned in the centre of the Syrian-controlled Beka'a Valley – and thus less than 35km from central Damascus – and populated by about 200,000 mostly Greek Orthodox Christians, Zahle was surrounded by mountains reaching up to 2,500 metres. The highest peak in the area is Mount Sannine, about 11km north-west of the city. By that

point in the Lebanese Civil War, there was next to no fighting in Zahle. While it is arguable that minor clashes between Christian residents and Palestinian militants did occur in mid and late 1976, once the ADF entered the country the Syrians treated Zahle with respect, while the Palestinians kept their distance. Consequently, no troops were stationed inside the city. Instead, the headquarters of the ADF was established in Chtoura, south-west of Zahle – where two commando battalions and one tank battalion were also stationed – and the Syrian Army concentrated on protecting the nearby Beirut–Damascus road. However, while securing the area, the Syrians failed to hold the peak of Mount Sannine, atop of which the LF constructed a fortified position known as the 'French Chamber'. This overlooked the entire Beka'a Valley, the Syrian side of Jebel Sheikh (Mount Hermon) and the Israeli-occupied Golan Heights in an easterly and south-easterly direction, and Jounieh – another Christian enclave – to the north-west. Below the mountain, the Lebanese armed forces had no presence in Zahle: the only formation there was the Hannache Group, a remnant of the Tigers militia, which was now supported by Syria and took over the local offices of the NLP in December 1980. Therefore, Gemayel infiltrated one of his 'commando' units along goat trails over Mount Sannine and ordered them to harass the Syrians.

On 19 December, a BRDM-2 armoured car of the Syrian Arab Army was hit by an RPG-7 and all five occupants killed. Having no idea who fired the shot, the Syrians imposed a 48-hour ultimatum upon the population of the city to turn out those responsible – or face the consequences. To demonstrate their intentions, the Syrians deployed their T-54/55s, commandos and artillery around Zahle, reinforced by elements of Fatah and the SSNP. With there being no response by the time the ultimatum expired, the Syrians shelled Haouch el-Omaraa Bulevard in the south, and al-Ma'allaqa and al-Hemmar districts on the eastern side of the city centre on 21 December. There followed a brief interruption during the next day, as under international pressure a ceasefire agreement had been reached. However, Gemayel's combatants then killed a Syrian soldier, and when the LF combatants refused to carry out the demand that they leave the city, the shelling resumed. The Syrians only stopped once Gemayel's men, under severe pressure from the local inhabitants, finally decided to withdraw (once again along goat trails over Mount Sannine) on 26 December. But by this time the damage had been done: not only were relations between the Christians of Zahle and the Syrians ruined, but Bashir Gemayel declared in negotiations with the Israelis that the city was under siege and 'in danger of being overrun by Syrian commandos'.

… TO THE ROAD TO ZAHLE

To underline his assessment and knowing the Syrian tactics for such situations – the essence of which was to surround and besiege the area of interest, and then shell it with artillery – Gemayel decided to repeat the exercise in January 1981. Once again, a unit of about 80 militants marched to Zahle along mountain trails. Upon arrival, they filed an encouraging report: the Syrians had blocked the roads towards the north but left the roads south open, while the mountain paths were hard going but passable for infantry. Most importantly, the unit reported that about 1,500 local men were armed and ready to fight the Syrians, but in need of leadership and ammunition.

Gemayel reacted promptly. In early February, a small number of RPG-7s, at least one 106mm recoilless rifle, ammunition and reinforcements were smuggled into the city from the south by trucks carrying food. Much more followed, with a column of 120 LF combatants commanded by Joe Edde, who reached Zahle carrying mortars and their bombs. By 9 February, the French Chamber on Mount Sannine was expanded into a communication relay between Zahle and Gemayel's HQ in Beirut. Due to the cold and wind, the conditions on the mountain peak were extreme, and even the alpine equipment acquired from abroad was not always of help. All the supplies – every single bullet, every can of beans and most of the water – had to be carried uphill by hand. It was only towards the end of the month that the LF acquired a single RATRAC snowcat vehicle, and with its help, and that of a few dozers that were active only by night, began constructing a clandestine road into Zahle. This was used to infiltrate 100 former combatants of the Guardians of the Cedars militia led by Kayrouz Barakat into Zahle.

POSITIONS

Inside the city of Zahle, Gemayel's men began constructing fortifications and trenches – mostly by night because the city was monitored (even if not particularly carefully) by Syrian troops deployed in the surrounding mountains. Gradually, a concentric system of defences emerged, starting with observation posts on nearby mountains, all linked by footpaths. A second circle consisted of a concealed line of trenches along the outskirts of the city, connected by communication trenches. Finally, key positions in Zahle were fortified and neighbourhood defences organised for every district, while Barakat's Guardians of the Cedars militia had heavily mined all the approaches to the city and, on 1 March 1981, completed the construction of a land-line telephone cable connecting them directly to the headquarters in Beirut. By now, the defences of Zahle were organised in four sectors (which later became six):

- Mountains: Qa'a el-Rim – Wadi al-A'arayech – High Mountain
- East: al-Midane – Houch az-Zara'ani – Barbara
- South: Tel Omara – Ma'allaqa – Industrial Zone
- West: ar-Rasiya – Bar Eliyas – Tel Shiha

Starting from 15 March, the LF Christian militia began redeploying its artillery and stocks of ammunition closer to the city: reportedly, S-65 helicopters of the IDF/AF were used to help move M50 howitzers to the hilltops of Oyoun el-Siman and Fagra, and then to Mount Sannine, and Israeli officers pre-selected targets and calculated ranges with the help of intelligence collected by their UAVs. Artillery was to play a major role in the defence plan, and the Lebanese Forces deployed eight mortar teams – including two teams operating 120mm tubes, one 4.7-in., two 82mm and one 81mm – in Wadi Casino, north-east of the city. All the new positions were carefully concealed in order to avoid their detection by SyAAF reconnaissance aircraft, which made regular overflights. Anti-tank assets included one jeep-

Over time, the Lebanese Forces in Zahle managed to repair – or simply requisitioned – several vehicles and convert them into 'technicals' through the installation of heavy machine guns. This photograph shows an example with a ZPU-1 (left) and an ex-US Army/ex-Lebanese Army truck with an S-60 57mm anti-aircraft gun (second from left). (via Jamal Itani)

EAGLES VERSUS MiGs: TAKE 4

The Treaty of Friendship between Moscow and Damascus, signed in October 1980, had two results indirectly related to the developments in Lebanon. One was the arrival of additional Soviet advisors, including a number of air warfare and air defence specialists. While the latter worked with the SyAADF, those assigned to the SyAAF were led by Lieutenant General Sokolov (a veteran of the Second World War) and included Lieutenant General Babenko (former Deputy Commander of the Baku Air Defence District of the Soviet Air Defence Force), Major General Ulchenko and Colonel Viktor Babich, one of most prominent aerial warfare theoreticians of the General Staff of the Soviet Armed Forces. Babich supervised about a dozen officers assigned to each of the SyAAF brigades with the task of improving the training of their pilots, developing new tactics to counter the IDF/AF and planning future operations. After studying the latest SyAAF experiences, they concluded that neither the MiG-21 nor MiG-23MS had a serious chance in one-against-one aerial combat against F-15s, but that the new US-made fighter should instead be fought by groups of MiGs following pre-planned, well-rehearsed scenarios, aided by flying at low altitudes and employing terrain masking.[2]

Brand-new MiG-25PDs were used to try these new tactics. The first unit equipped with the new type – reportedly No. 5 Squadron – was declared operational in December 1980. Its first commander was either Lieutenant Colonel Ali Sueleiman Ibrahim or Lieutenant Colonel Junaid, and jets flown by them and their pilots could reach speeds of more than Mach 2, were equipped with the powerful, jamming-resistant RP-25 Smerch-A2 radar and armed with semi-active radar homing R-40RD and infra-red homing R-40TD medium-range air-to-air missiles (ASCC/NATO-codename 'AA-6 Acrid'). These missiles had a maximum engagement range of between 35 and 50km (19–27 miles), which was more than enough to outrange AIM-7Fs in the Israeli arsenal. On the negative side, the Smerch-A2 was a low-PRF radar, optimised for attacks on high-flying bombers: as such, it had only a depressed-angle capability, which meant that it could not engage targets flying lower than the MiG-25. With this fact being well-known to the US and Israeli military intelligence, it was to become the biggest weakness in all the aerial battles fought by this type over Lebanon.

A cross-examination of published Israeli and Russian accounts of the clash from 13 February 1981 enables the following reconstruction. A single F-4E(S) or RF-4E from No. 119 Squadron of the IDF/AF launched from Tel Nov AB for a reconnaissance sortie over Lebanon. Around 1316 hours local time, the jet was detected by Syrian early warning radars while at an altitude of 13,000 metres (42,650ft) and speed of 1,000km/h, heading in a northerly direction. Such a high-flying aircraft was an ideal target for the MiG-25PD, and one was scrambled from the T-4 AB. Around 1325 hours, the Syrian jet reached an altitude of 8,000 metres (26,246ft) and accelerated to Mach 1.5 while heading in the direction of Lebanon. The ground controller then made a major mistake: he ordered the pilot to power up his Smerch-A2 when 110km (68½ miles) away from the target. The Syrian pilot promptly locked on to the reconnaissance Phantom but was still outside his missile range. However, emissions from the Smerch radar provided the Israelis with plenty of time to recognise the incoming threat and to react accordingly. Moments later, the MiG-25 pilot reported his target disappearing in a large and growing 'spot' on his radar display. Apparently, the Phantom deployed a cloud of 'chaff': thin aluminium strips, cut to a length suitable to return a strong echo on Syrian radars and thus confuse their operators. To the Syrian ground control, the target now appeared to be descending: to retain it within the engagement envelope of the Smerch-2A, the controller ordered the MiG-25 to descend to an altitude of 5,000 metres (16,404ft). By 1327 hours, the Syrian jet had cut the range to about 50km (31 miles), at which point the Israelis activated their ECM and all contact between the MiG pilot and his ground control was lost. A few seconds later, the Syrian ground control detected an F-15 rapidly climbing from behind the mountains and turning to meet the MiG-25 head-on. Obviously, this was another ambush, with the Eagle approaching the combat zone at low altitude, in the radar 'shadow' of the Lebanese mountains. When the range was down to 25km, the F-15 pilot, Benny Zinker, fired an AIM-7F, followed by two more, from 17 and 12 miles away (27.4 and 19.3km, respectively). One of the missiles either proximity fused or hit the left wing of the MiG, causing it to flip into a spin. The pilot ejected and landed safely by parachute, still inside Syria. The F-15 had proven itself superior even against the latest – and supposedly most modern – interceptor of Soviet origin, only months after this had entered operational service

A nice view of F-15A serial 646, shortly after its arrival in Israel. The example flown by Yoram Peled when he shot down a Syrian MiG-21 on 27 June 1979, and then by Benjamin Zinker during the first clash with MiG-25s on 13 February 1981, wore the serial number 672. (IDF)

An SA.321K Super Frelon helicopter (serial 017) of No. 114 Squadron IDF/AF arriving at Jounieh, a stronghold of the Gemayels and the headquarters of the Lebanese Forces, in 1980. (Photo by Francois de Mulder)

to about 90. These were supported by a concentration of some 50 D-30 howitzers and M-46 guns, several batteries of BM-14 and BM-21 MRLS rockets and a strong concentration (about 50 tubes in total) of 160mm and 240mm mortars. These forces were deployed in three main positions around the city, all including high earthen berms and firing positions for tanks and artillery:

- north-west: Hazerta
- north-east: between the Berdawny River Bridge and Kark to the Khatib Hospital
- south-west: Houch el-Omara

Overall, by the end of March, the Syrian contingent of the ADF had about 5,700 troops in the Zahle area and could count on receiving reinforcements from Damascus by helicopter if necessary.

BATTLE OF THE BRIDGE

Once everything was ready, the Lebanese Forces and their local allies went into action. On 1 April, scouts informed Edde and Barakat that the Syrians were moving to secure the hills of Harkat and Hemmar. An RPG team was deployed to launch a counterattack, sneaking upon the enemy and, using one of its rocket-propelled grenades, destroying the bulldozer that had been digging tank berms. The Syrians reacted by shelling the area from which the attack came, buying time for their commandos to intervene. However, when the commandos attempted to reach Tel Chiha, they ran into an ambush and were pinned down. As evermore SyAA units moved towards the scene of the firefight, a chaotic battle developed in the direction of the Lady of Zahle shrine. The chaos was then exploited by one of the LF's mortar teams, which shelled the compound housing the ADF's main headquarters in Chtoura, while another squad mortared the Syrian Army's checkpoints protecting the bridge on the Bardouni River on the Beirut–Damascus road.

mounted 106mm recoilless rifle and two 107mm versions, along with several dozen RPG-7s. By the end of March, the defenders of Zahle commanded by Joe Edde numbered between 2,500 and 3,000, of which about 400 were LF members from outside the city.

Distracted by developments at home, the command of the ADF was slow in getting wind of what was going on inside Zahle. Moreover, once Khatib began moving reinforcements in that direction, the best parts of his 78th Armoured and 85th Mechanised Brigades (which included 47 MBTs) were withdrawn to Syria and replaced by poorly trained reservists. However, the commander of the ADF had to act, and once he realised the seriousness of the situation, Khatib took care to further reinforce his depleted assets. In a matter of days, the number of available MBTs was increased

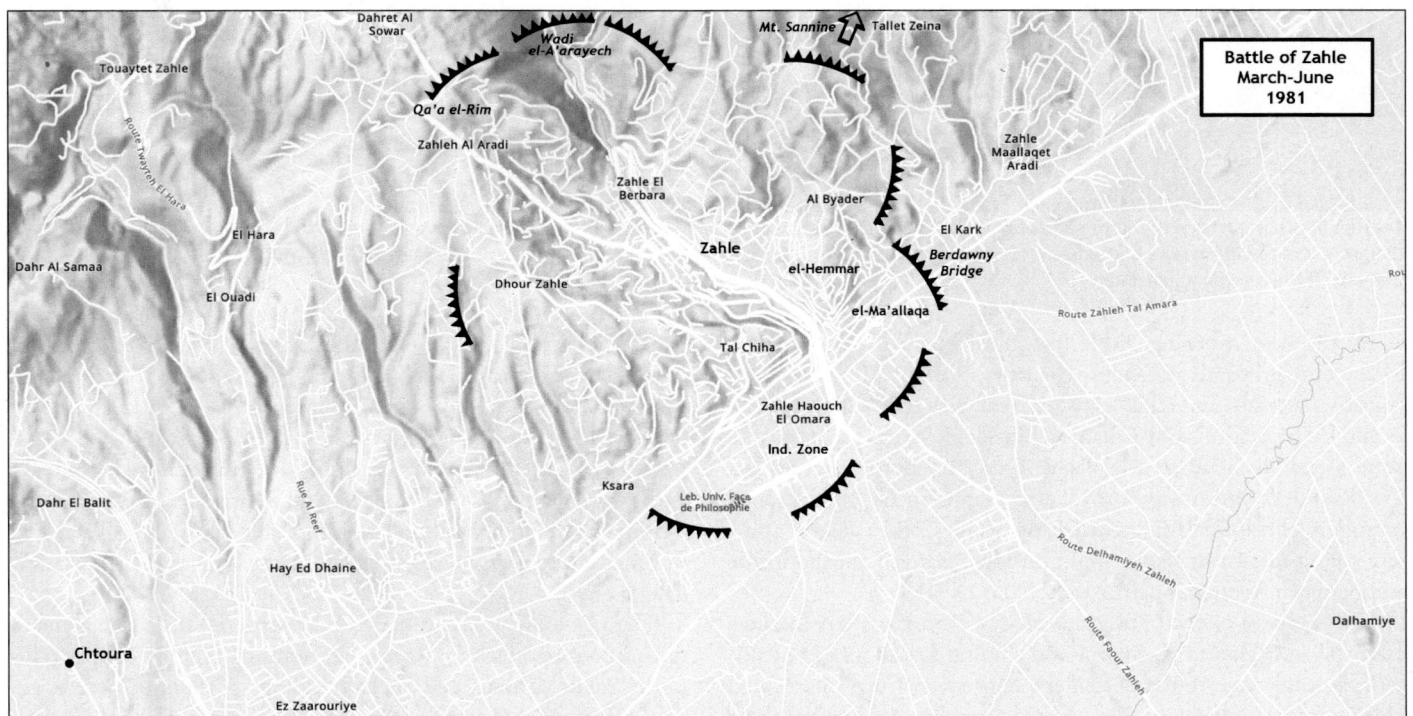

Map of LF and SyAA positions in and around Zahle as of late March and early April 1981. (Map by Tom Cooper)

A clandestinely taken photograph showing some of the wreckage left behind by the Syrians during the Battle of the Bridge in Zahle on 1 April 1981. In the foreground, a T-55 MBT is towing a disabled BMP-1 IFV. Visible in the background on the left is a burned-out T-55, and to the right is the T-55 that was driven off the road and abandoned by its crew with the engine still running. (via Jamal Itani)

Another photograph from the same series, taken slightly later and showing a Syrian VT-55 armoured recovery vehicle in the process of towing away a burned-out T-55. Visible in the background are another burned-out T-55 and the example that ran off the road. (via Jamal Itani)

Bridge. Preceded by a T-55 equipped with a mine-roller, the tank column moved without any infantry support – and ran straight into an LF ambush, as recalled by George Azzi, commander of the Haouch el-Omara garrison:

'The Syrians were advancing with tanks … but had no infantry elements to protect them from our B-7 shells, and were easy to hit, because the tanks were moving slowly like a person that sees only in one direction. [Deploying] tanks in the streets is of no benefit for a regular army, equipped and trained to fight in open spaces.'

As the first two T-54/55s drove down the Ma'allaqa road, they found themselves subjected to simultaneous attacks from multiple directions. Although no tank was completely destroyed, the panicked crews attempted to abandon their vehicles – only to be gunned down from close range. The second platoon of three tanks was ambushed shortly after: two were hit with the first shots, their crews jumping out and running away, while the other drove off the road and was abandoned with its engine still running. The sixth T-54/55 managed to advance and pass the bridge, but upon reaching the hospital junction its crew realised they were on their own and thus decided to return towards Kerak. On their way back, they fired blindly in the direction of the area where the other tanks had been knocked out or abandoned. The Syrian commander then rushed four additional tanks and BRDM-2s to the scene, but three of the MBTs and one armoured car were knocked out by RPGs, with most of their crews being killed.

After this success, the LF headquarters in Beirut rushed a team with two Milan ATGM-launchers and 24 missiles, led by Helmy ash-Shartouni and Habi Atallah, into Zahle via Wadi al-A'arayech. Another group carrying 20 additional missiles was to follow a few days later.

The next day, an emboldened Edde ordered his combatants to stage a counterattack on the Syrian outposts held by commandos in the Sakhr, Ghurra and Sekka buildings of the industrial zone. This effort was cut to pieces by Syrian snipers, who took a heavy toll on the Christians. While this was going on, the Syrians

By the next morning, Edde has re-established control of his forces and prepared defences. A team of about 70 combatants (mostly Assyrians and Chaldeans), armed with RPG-2s and RPG-7s and led by Jean 'Cobra' Ohanion, was deployed in the industrial zone along the road to Ma'allaqa. Near the Berdawny Bridge, the defenders commanded by Pierre Hajj – including seasoned members of the Phalange, Guardians of the Cedars, Tigers and a few youngsters from Zahle – split into five teams deployed inside and between homes along the road.

The Syrians opened their advance with an artillery barrage of Ma'allaqa, Madina as-Snaiya and the industrial zone, but this caused no damage to the defenders. Moreover, from intercepted radio communications, Edde learned that the Syrian Army was about to re-deploy a tank force from Kerak to the Berdawny

A view down the Ma'allaqa road, with two knocked out or abandoned Syrian T-55s. (via Jamal Itani)

continued their barrage of Zahle, inflicting numerous civilian casualties and eventually prompting the LF's artillery to respond: the latter shelled concentrations of Syrian Army troops at several positions around the city. After sunset, the Syrians launched a further tank attack, but once again undertaken without infantry support, this was easily beaten back with the loss of T-54/55s knocked out by RPG teams operating from higher structures along the Kerak road. Finally, in an attempt to distract the ADF's attention away from Zahle, Gemayel ordered the LF into an attack on West Beirut, which in turn drew heavy shelling by Syrian and Palestinian artillery. Edde and his aides then tried to arrange an influx of reinforcements and supplies, but with the Syrians in control of all the regular roads and managing to prevent the paving of the LF-constructed route over Mount Sannine, everything still had to be carried by hand. Nevertheless, early on 4 April, a group of 90 LF combatants led by Nabil at-Tun and carrying arms and ammunition managed to reach Zahle after an 11-hour march over the mountains. However, they were barely inside the city when the first ceasefire was negotiated. Thus ended the first Battle of Zahle, best known among the Christians of Lebanon as the Tank Massacre or Battle of the Bridge. The battle's outcome was crystal clear: the Syrians had not only failed to breach Zahle's defences, but lost about 20 armoured vehicles, including 15 tanks. Although successful in defence and meanwhile reinforced, the LF suffered heavy losses in its counterattacks, leaving Edde deeply concerned about the growing shortage of combatants and supplies.

LOSS OF THE HILLS

The ceasefire of 4 April held for only a few hours, as both sides soon began exchanging artillery fire. Furious about what was going on inside Zahle, Khatib concentrated every single one of his BM-14s and BM-21s to fire rockets into the city. Shartouni's and Atallah's teams shot back with Milan ATGMs: although hits were claimed on several MBTs deployed in the el-Hammar area, Ben Elias and the Lady of Zahle shrine, the actual results remain unknown. Nevertheless, it is certain that they would have left a strong impression upon the Syrians, who became gravely concerned about the effects of the Milan missiles. During the following days, the LF headquarters in Zahle began broadcasting fake radio messages about deployments of Milan teams to different

sectors under Syrian pressure – without actually doing so. On more than one occasion, however, such deception was sufficient to persuade the enemy to withdraw its T-54/55s. Henceforth, they tended instead to deploy their MBTs as self-propelled artillery. That said, Khatib had meanwhile reinforced his artillery and began deploying it for counterbattery fire at the LF's pieces. As soon as this was shown to be successful, he launched attacks by heliborne commandos on Lebanese Forces' positions in the hills around Zahle to ensure the total isolation of the city. Supported by their artillery and strikes by Mi-8 helicopters armed with UB-16-57 pods for 57mm unguided rockets, the Syrians first secured Niha hill, north-east of Zahle, before assaulting al-Maghair hill, east of the city. A see-saw battle for the latter peak ensued, in which the Christians first lost, then recovered their position, but were eventually forced to withdraw the following night.

After the loss of al-Maghair hill, the LF commanders inside Zahle had no illusions about their ability to hold out against the Syrians. Clearly outgunned and outnumbered from the start, they lacked the troops to hold all their positions in necessary strength. Nevertheless, they decided to stay and fight. Indeed, when the Syrians assaulted Chaste hill – a position controlling the main supply route via Wadi al-Arayesh – early on 6 April, the defenders managed to repel them using hand-grenades and RPGs. The same exercise was repeated on Armata hill shortly later. Disappointed by their lack of success, the Syrians began hammering both positions with artillery fire and a string of helicopter strikes before attacking again and securing the peaks of Chaste and Armata early on 7 April. With this, all the hills around Zahle apart from Sannine were under Syrian control.

SUDDEN END

The success of its troops and the need to reorganise and replenish, encouraged Damascus to accept an offer for a 48-hour-long ceasefire negotiated by Syrian Foreign Minister Abdul Halim Khaddam and President Sarkis. Moreover, none other than Hafez al-Assad offered a compromise: the siege would be lifted if the Phalangists withdrew. Bashir Gemayel promptly rejected the proposal and spurred his men to fight on, explaining to them that the Syrian strongman was demanding their unconditional surrender, with responsibility for security in Zahle to be taken over by the Lebanese Army, under the supervision of the ADF. Meanwhile, to the Israelis he presented the situation as a massacre of the Christian population and complained about air raids by Syrian helicopters. The Israeli leadership received Gemayel's reports with scepticism, and IDF officers sent to inspect the situation in the nearby Christian enclave of Jounieh reported back that the LF leader was exaggerating. Nevertheless, the Israeli government made more promises, increasing Bashir's confidence. The fighting thus went on, even if there was little left to fight for. After

TOP SECRET: PART 2

During the Battle of Zahle, Israel intensified the secret delivery of arms and ammunition to Gemayel's Lebanese Forces to a frequency of one roundtrip every four days. For example, on 21 April 1981, in Operation Leather Sandal 5, INS *Ashdod* delivered several trucks loaded with ammunition directly on the beach near Jounieh, despite a heavy storm that caused one of the vehicles to roll into the sea together with its load. Another load of trucks stuffed full with firearms and ammunition was delivered on 28 April by INS *Achziv* (escorted by the Sa'ar-3-

class INS *Hanit*) in Operation Leather Sandal 6, while Leather Sandal 7 was run only a day later. Concerned about a possible Syrian air strike, escorts were reinforced after the Israeli downing of two Syrian helicopters. On 11 May, INS *Bat-Sheva*, escorted by the Sa'ar-3-class INS *Sufa* and Sa'ar-4-class INS *Atzmaut*, and two Dabur-class patrol boats ran the last delivery to Jounieh. Their radars detected several aerial contacts, but the Syrians never approached the area or attempted to interfere with the missions.[3]

The Sa'ar-4-class corvette INS *Komamiut* in August 1978. By 1981, vessels of this kind were regularly escorting ships delivering armament, ammunition and supplies to Gemayel's Lebanese Forces. (Clandestine Immigration and Naval Museum, Haifa)

heavy combat along the axis al-Mala'aqa–Houch–el-Omara, the Syrian troops overcame the LF's resistance, securing the area and forcing surviving enemy fighters into their last two strongholds. Following another short ceasefire to enable representatives of the International Committee of the Red Cross to deliver medication and evacuate wounded civilians, Syrian commandos, supported by artillery and Gazelle and Mi-8 helicopters, secured most of the city on the morning of 10 April. During the following night, Gemayel – fresh from a meeting with al-Khuli, the head of the notorious AFID, and concerned that the Syrians were about to launch an all-out attack on the remaining Christian enclaves – addressed the surviving LF combatants in Zahle in typical fashion:

> Because the road is still open for a few hours only … if you leave, you will save your lives and the fall of the city will be certain and this will be the end of our resistance … if you stay, you will find yourselves without ammunition, without medicine, without

bread, and maybe without water, your task will be to coordinate the internal resistance and defend the identity of the Lebanese Beka'a and the identity of Lebanon, and by that you will give a meaning to our six years [of] war. If you decide to stay, know one thing, that heroes die and they don't surrender.

Joe Edde responded that they were staying. Thus, the battle went on, with the Syrians now subjecting Zahle to relentless shelling and air strikes by Gazelle and Mi-8 helicopters forward-deployed at Ryak AB. The attacks went on until 15 April, when a fresh ceasefire was agreed through US mediation.

NIGHT PRAYER[4]

That the Lebanese Civil War was a particularly ironic affair – especially when one considers specific statements and actions of the government of Prime Minister Begin – was confirmed around the time the Battle of Zahle was reaching its high point.

While making statements for the press that the policy of pre-emptive raids into Lebanon, introduced two years earlier, was a 'giant success' that had 'greatly reduced terrorist incidents', Begin ordered the IDF to launch its own next raid. Originally planned in the wake of earlier operations into the same area, the resulting Operation Night Prayer was a follow-up that included a task force of about 200 troops, airlifted for an assault on the Palestinian positions around the village of Dayr el-Zahrani, about a kilometre south of the Zahrani River and some 20km from the Israeli border. Interestingly, the primary aim of the operation was to knock out two T-34/85 tanks of the PLO that had been harassing the SLA for some time, and thus force the Palestinians to withdraw all of their armour from the proximity of Haddad's enclave. This time, nearly all the assault elements were drawn from the Parachute Brigade (commanded by Colonel Yoram 'Ya-Ya' Yair):

- Task Force North: Forward Controller Team (commanded by Yair)
- Task Force South: Forward Controller Team (commanded by Saul Mofaz)
- Combat Team from the 50th Parachute Battalion (tasked with blocking the road from Habbouch village in the south)
- Combat Team from the 202nd Parachute Battalion (tasked with destruction of the two T-34/85s)
- Combat Team from the 890th Parachute Battalion (tasked with demolition of several artillery positions and adjacent buildings)
- Combat Team from the Parachute Brigade Reconnaissance Unit
- Combat Team from the Parachute Brigade Anti-Tank Unit (tasked with blocking the route to the north and demolition of buildings)
- Combat Team of the Unit 269 (commanded by Moshe Ya'alon tasked with destruction of a tented camp)
- Combat Team of the Parachute Brigade Engineering Unit (tasked with demolition of a bunker)

Additionally, a 32-strong team from the Reconnaissance Unit of the 1st Golani Infantry Brigade (commanded by Major Goni Hernik) was tasked with ambushing PLO vehicles along the road from Nabatiyah to Saida, about 1.5km west of Dayr el-Zahrani. This combat team was airlifted to the target zone first, late in the evening of 9 April. Upon landing, it split into four sections that blocked the road and, within minutes, engaged and destroyed two vehicles.

The main body of the Parachute Task Force was flown in by S-65 helicopters, and then marched to their objectives, at some of which the Palestinians offered bitter resistance, while others were found to be empty. By the morning of 10 April, all objectives were secured, with the two T-34/85s completely destroyed, and the Israelis then quickly withdrew. During the course of Operation Night Prayer the Israelis lost one man killed and a dozen wounded, while Palestinian casualties remain unknown.

SHOWDOWN OVER ZAHLE

During the ceasefire negotiated on 15 April, Lieutenant General Khatib continued bringing in Syrian reinforcements and supplies, and ordered his troops to secure Kaa' el-Rim, a small town near Zahle. When the local defenders repelled their attack, the Syrians captured nearby water tanks and blew them up, hoping to cut off the defenders of the – now completely ruined – Zahle from

their water supply. However, employees of the local water supply authority restored a back-up water tank from the old network, and the supply was soon restored, the area around the old water tank having been heavily mined. Nevertheless, the defenders, now critically short of ammunition and food, were becoming desperate. To add to their misery, on 24 April, Khatib deployed one of his special forces battalions for a heliborne attack on Mount Senin. The assault began early on the following day, when the Syrians quickly overran the defenders of the French Chamber. Desperate to recover Mount Senin and reopen the way into Zahle, the Lebanese Forces launched several counterattacks, but all were repelled. Indeed, during the following days, the Syrian commandos continued advancing, and eventually secured most of the mountain. Predictably, when finding no other solution, Bashir Gemayel called for help from Israel.

At this point, the Syrians seem to have made a serious strategic mistake. Following extensive studies of earlier aerial combats with Israeli F-15s, they launched their fifth attempt to challenge Israel's aerial superiority on 26 April, this time following a pre-planned, well-rehearsed scenario, with the help of terrain masking. As a first move, a pair of MiG-23MS fighters from No. 99 Squadron were launched to distract Israeli attention with a demonstrative flight at high altitude and high speed towards Beirut. As soon as F-15s turned in pursuit, the Syrians brought in another pair of MiG-23MS jets low in between the Lebanese hills, and then had them attack a formation of A-4 Skyhawks involved in dive-bombing PLO armoured formations in the Sidon area. Reportedly, two Skyhawks were shot down by R-13Ms.[5]

As far as is known, the Israelis never found this claim worthy of comment. This is unsurprising, considering even their most prominent historians tend 'not to know' about any kind of IDF/AFs losses caused by Syrian interceptors, regardless of what war was being fought between the two countries. This makes it impossible to gauge whether any attack by SyAAF interceptors – successful or not – on 26 April had any influence upon subsequent developments. That said, it is certain that the AMAN and the IDF in general were monitoring the situation in Zahle carefully, but – except through supporting the redeployment of the LF's artillery and selling it ammunition – they did not become actively involved. Of course, the top ranks of the IDF and Begin's government were kept informed about developments. The Prime Minister of Israel was in favour of Gemayel, and insisted on 'preventing a genocide of Christians' – but his generals were not the least optimistic. Available Israeli accounts all stress that the Chief-of-Staff of the IDF, General Eitan, and the Chief-of-Staff Northern Command IDF, General Ben-Gal, did not trust the self-imposed Maronite leader, and did not like the idea of a confrontation with the Syrians under such conditions as prevailed. General Yehoshua Saguy, head of the AMAN, had figured out that Gemayel's intention was actually aimed at provoking an Israeli military intervention. To sort out such and similar disagreements, and decide what to do next, Begin's cabinet sat down to discuss matters on 28 April – including Eitan's proposal to intercept and shoot down Syrian helicopters involved in the Battle of Zahle. Saguy and several ministers argued against such action, explaining that the Syrians would certainly then bring their SAMs into Lebanon, in turn limiting the freedom of movement of the IDF/AF. However, authorisation for an operation against SyAAF helicopters was eventually granted and Eitan apparently left the room to order the IDF/AF to prepare for just such an action.[6]

FOREGOING INTERCEPT

Whether Eitan ordered the Air Force to prepare an intercept or *actually ordered it to fly it*, remains unclear. What is certain is that only minutes later, two F-16s from No. 117 'First Jet' Squadron were scrambled from Ramat David AB in northern Israel. Ground control advised both pilots – Ze'ev Raz and Rafi Berkovich – to remain at low altitude and proceed towards Haifa. They crossed the Mediterranean coast, turned north/north-east and climbed to an altitude of 20,000ft (6,096 metres) upon reaching Beirut. After a few minutes on station, ground control advised them of targets at low altitude in the Ryak AB area, and the F-16s swooped down towards the east. Raz's radar malfunctioned, but Berkovich locked on to a Mi-8 from a range of 25 miles (40km). After descending to about 5,000ft (1,524 metres), Berkovich attacked first, firing a single AIM-9L missile – which missed the low-flying helicopter. The two F-16s passed by their target and pulled up, only to receive a warning from their ground control as a pair of MiGs were approaching the area and now only 20 miles (32km) away. Repositioning, Berkovich attacked the Mi-8 from a 45-degree dive and sprayed it with some 250 20mm rounds. The helicopter caught fire and crashed to the ground south of Zahle, killing everybody on board. Shortly after, Raz sighted another helicopter low over Ryak AB, and shot it down using a single AIM-9L. The entire affair was over by the time Eitan returned to the cabinet session to inform a startled Begin and his government that the IDF/AF had just shot down two Syrian Mi-8s.[7]

The belated, but highly effective Israeli action now presented Hafez al-Assad with a choice: he could withdraw from Lebanon and expose a border a mere 30km from central Damascus to the Israelis, or he could escalate the crisis. Predictably, he opted for the latter solution: while refusing any further US mediation attempts and offering Gemayel the opportunity to withdraw peacefully from Zahle, the following night he ordered the deployment of an air defence brigade of the SyAADF, including three battalions (three 'SAM sites') of 2K12 Kub (ASCC/NATO-codename 'SA-6 Gainful') and one of S-75 (ASCC/NATO-codename 'SA-2 Guideline') SAMs into the Beka'a Valley. This unit was supported by an air defence regiment equipped with anti-aircraft artillery, two radio-technical battalions and two electronic warfare battalions, which moved into positions that had been prepared by Syrian engineers in late March. Two additional air defence brigades took up positions along the border between Lebanon and Syria. Furthermore, in full sight of Israeli reconnaissance jets and UAVs, the 115th Missile Brigade,

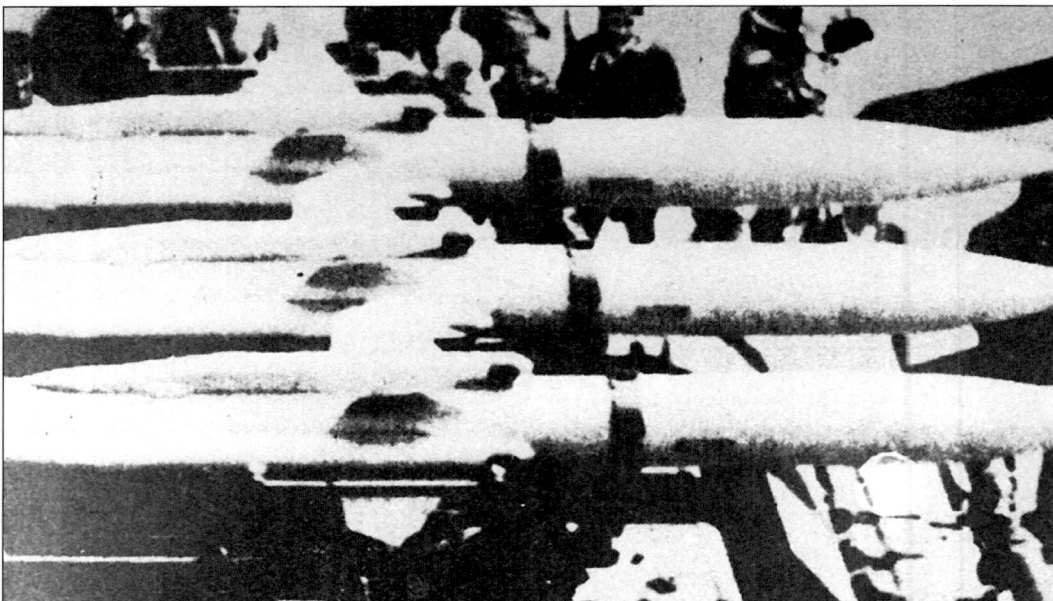

A rare photograph of Syrian-operated SA-6s, on display during a military parade in Damascus in the mid-1970s. (Albert Grandolini Collection)

F-16A serial number 112 of the No. 117 'First Jet' Squadron, shortly after delivery, while still wearing the serial applied at the factory in Fort Worth. (IDF)

Another view of the same F-16A, again shortly after delivery to Israel. This jet scored the first ever kill for this prolific type when downing a Syrian Mi-8 helicopter over the Ryak area in Lebanon on 28 April 1981. (IDF)

One of the first photographs taken of Syrian SA-6s deployed in the Zahle area. Visible are three 3M9M missiles, which were always installed on launch rails on top of the 3M9 transporter-erector-launcher (TEL). (Albert Grandolini Collection)

equipped with Soviet-made R-17E (ASCC/NATO-codename 'SS-1c Scud-B') ballistic missiles, was ordered into a position north-west of Damascus.

Just as predictably, the Israelis quickly forgot about the siege of Zahle and promptly began complaining about this Syrian threat against what, by that time, was their well-established aerial superiority in what was actually sovereign Lebanese airspace. Indeed, Begin went as far as to loudly threaten the destruction of the missiles should they not be withdrawn: Assad adamantly refused. Predictably, the IDF/AF received orders to prepare for the destruction of the missiles.

7

UNPROVOKED ONSLAUGHT

To say that the downing of the two SyAAF helicopters and Operation Night Prayer were entirely unnecessary and counterproductive provocations that brought the situation between Israel and Syria in Lebanon close to boiling point would be an understatement. However, it was not the last such decision: on the contrary, over the following weeks and months, the Begin government continued making demands and decisions that were not only bordering on the absurd, but had murderous consequences for many Lebanese and then Israeli civilians for decades to come.[1]

OVERTURE

In retaliation for the Israeli Operation Night Prayer, the PLO launched a small-scale rocket attack on several settlements in Upper Galilee on 10 April 1981. While these caused no casualties or damage, the IDF/AF was ordered to hit back at a Palestinian camp outside Ras el-Sa'adiyat, about 15km north of Sidon. The Palestinians responded with an artillery barrage of the Christian enclave in southern Lebanon: although Israel was not hit, the entire population of the Metula area was ordered to spend the following night in shelters. When Israel did not retaliate, the PLO redirected its attention: on 18 April, its artillery heavily shelled IDF positions in the Marjayoun area of Lebanon, while its combatants planted several mines and improvised explosive devices (IEDs). Two of Haddad's SLA armoured personnel carriers were knocked out by them during the following days, and when the infantry gathered around them, the Palestinians detonated another IED, killing three men and wounding two. Following the usual Israeli behaviour in such cases, the SLA reacted by shelling PLO positions in the Sidon area: however, a number of their shells hit populated areas, killing more than 20 civilians. On 20 April, IDF engineers working on de-mining the area around Marjayoun came under mortar fire from Beaufort Castle, losing one officer killed and a soldier wounded (according to another version of this incident, casualties were caused by another mine or IED). Later the same day, fighter-bombers of the IDF/AF bombed both the Beaufort and Nabatiyah areas, and there followed a heavy exchange of artillery fire between the PLO and the SLA, while several 122mm rockets from Palestinian BM-21s landed inside Israel. The final action of the day saw warships of the IDF/Sea Corps shelling targets in the Sidon area, being assisted by fighter-bombers that dropped illumination flares.

MISSILE CRISIS

Busy in Zahle, the Syrians reacted only with the above-mentioned interception of A-4s over Damour on 26 April. On the next day, the IDF flew several air strikes, one of which targeted the PFLP-GC's base equipped with MRLS rockets and protected by anti-aircraft artillery about 2.5km north-east of Nabatiyah. Another struck the PLO base in el-Hlaliyeh and its handful of tanks and tank transports about 3km south-east of Sidon, while a third strike bombed the PFLP base in Hamidiyeh, 5km north-east of Tyre. According to PLO reports, about 40 Palestinians were killed or wounded, provoking the organisation to retaliate with a volley of BM-21 rockets fired at Upper Galilee, while their artillery shelled the IDF positions in the Marjayoun area. In return, Haddad's artillery bombarded Jarmaq and the Nabatiyah areas. On 30 April, Begin ordered Eitan to destroy the three SA-6 sites that were in the Beka'a Valley at the time. A strike was scheduled for 1100 hours but had to be postponed to 1300 hours and then to 1500 hours because of bad weather. Eventually, it was postponed to the following day. On the same day, Assad requested help from Moscow, offering the port of Tartous and the T-4 Air Base (colloquially 'Tiyas' or 'Teefor') in exchange for the deployment of one aviation brigade and three air defence brigades to Syria, along with accelerated deliveries of MiG-23s. Moscow in turn contacted Washington, prompting the new administration of US President Ronald Reagan to become involved and demand both the Israelis and Syrians avoid further escalation until its representatives could negotiate. For the next few days, US Secretary of State Alexander Haig toured the Middle East, including Israel, demanding that Begin hold off from launching any military response and to let the USA deal with the crisis. The Soviets joined in the peace effort, and their ambassador to Damascus, Vladimir Yukhin, announced that Syrian troops would halt their operations in Lebanon, while the Soviet ambassador in the USA denied any involvement there of Soviet personnel in operations.

However, by the time Reagan appointed retired diplomat Philip Habib as his special envoy and dispatched him to the Middle East, the Syrians had announced military exercises near the Lebanese border on 4 May. Begin's cabinet promptly reacted with another ultimatum, demanding an unconditional withdrawal of the SAM sites from the Beka'a Valley. Unsurprisingly, Hafez al-Assad formally refused, announcing his readiness to fight back if attacked. Nothing of substance happened for the next few days, as Habib – of Maronite Christian origins and with a solid background in crisis management – ran his shuttle diplomacy between Beirut, Damascus and Tel Aviv. Understanding the fragility of the situation, he suggested a withdrawal of LF troops from Zahle and their replacement by the Lebanese Army, with the Syrian SAMs to remain in place but with an agreement that they never fire at Israeli aircraft, and the Israelis to guarantee they would not attack the Syrian contingent of the ADF. By 11 May, nearly everybody had agreed to Habib's proposals, when Begin gave a speech in the Knesset, the Israeli parliament, revealing interesting details about the deployment of the SyAADF SAMs:

> I will report to the Knesset on the number of missiles which have been stationed in Lebanon and the Lebanese–Syrian border. In Lebanon itself, there are presently five SA-6 sites. On the border, there are another four to six sites. Along the Lebanese–Syrian border there are already two SA-2 sites (until two days ago there was only one battery of this type). Along the Lebanese–Syrian border there are already two SA-3 sites as of this morning (two days ago there was only one). There are also SA-9 sites exported by Libya to Lebanon and they are manned by Libyans. All told, there are 14 SAM sites.

A day later, on 12 May, the first shots since the beginning of the 'missile crisis' were fired: on two occasions, the Syrian SAM sites deployed along the border opened fire at Israeli aircraft that violated Lebanese airspace. In neither case did the missiles cause any damage, despite Syrian claims about one aircraft being shot down (such reports subsequently increased by the Soviets to 'one F-15 and three F-16s').[2] Syrian state TV rushed to show fragments of wreckage as evidence of success, but what was shown instead were parts of a Ryan Model 124 Firebee UAV shot down over Homs on 7 October 1979. All that was actually downed was one of the much smaller, Israeli-made Scout UAVs.

On 14 May, Syrian SAM sites deployed in the Beka'a Valley fired no less than six missiles: three shot down a Model 124 of the IDF/AF's No. 200 'First UAV' Squadron that was underway at high altitude, while the other three failed to bring down an RF-4E.

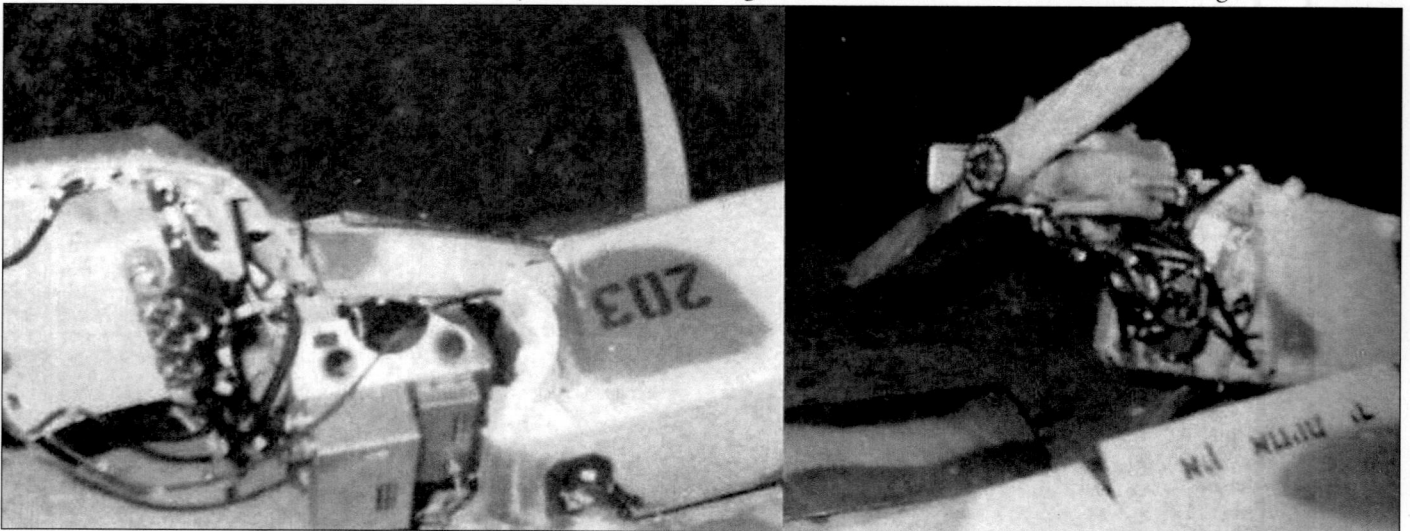

Wreckage of the IAI Scout shot down by Syrian SAMs on 12 May 1981. (Efim Sandler Collection)

Wreckage of the Israeli-made Telem UAV shot down by Syrian air defences on 14 May 1981. Clearly visible on what was left of the wings are traces of the shrapnel from a SAM that proximity fused. (Efim Sandler Collection)

On the same day, another Firebee was intercepted by a MiG-21 at 40,000ft (12,192 metres) over Lebanon, but the jet stalled, forcing the pilot to eject. A week later, on 21 May, the IAI Scout UAV made its operational debut over the Beka'a Valley and transmitted live images of a Syrian SA-6 SAM site in real time, but the Syrians began adapting to the new threat and shot down two of the Israeli UAVs on 22 and 25 May.

By then, Habib's negotiations were in a state of stalemate, for while the Palestinians were ready to accept a ceasefire, Begin continued issuing new threats on a daily basis, while the Syrian contingent of the ADF continued hammering positions of the Lebanese Forces in Zahle and East Beirut. Meanwhile, the USA and the USSR were blaming each other over who had triggered the conflict. Consequently, Habib ended his tour and returned to Washington on 27 May, announcing that he had succeeded in calming down the situation but was unsure who would make the next step.

ASSAD'S BLUFF

Meant as a warning for Begin not to intervene and expand the scope of the conflict, Assad's decision to deploy SAMs in Lebanon caused a 20-day-long exchange of threats and counterthreats, with some old-fashioned 'sabre rattling'. Intended as a demonstration of force, Assad's actions proved effective primarily due to an intervention from Washington which stopped an Israeli attack on SA-6s only minutes before it was launched. In turn, in another of his ironic decisions (especially so considering his earlier bragging about the success of his doctrine against the PLO), Begin instead ordered the IDF/AF into a new aerial offensive against the Palestinians. Finally, having achieved what he wanted, Bashir Gemayel agreed to an Arab-mediated withdrawal of his surviving troops from Zahle and their replacement by troops of the Lebanese Army. The battle thus ended in late June 1981.

However, in military terms, Assad's actions were both a farce and a bluff. The SA-6s were deployed inside a valley surrounded by high mountain peaks, from where their radar coverage and effective engagement envelope were extremely limited. They were on their own – and thus extremely vulnerable to air strikes – for several days after their arrival. Only then were the Syrians capable of linking them with their integrated air defence systems (IADS)

covering south-western Syria, which was done with help of a Soviet-made Vektor-2VE automatic tactical management system. Measured by Soviet standards of 1979, this was still a modern, computer-supported system. Introduced to Soviet service in 1973, the Vektor-2 was capable of simultaneously tracking 82 targets while controlling the work of 14 SAM sites and 12 manned interceptors against targets within a radius of about 250km. As such, it was even more advanced than the two Vektor-1MEs in service with the SyAADF since 1973, each of which could track 41 targets at the same time. However, its coupling with the latter was a clumsy solution, even more so because of the rugged terrain of Lebanon, which blocked the 'view' of Syrian radars towards the west and south. This resulted in a situation in the SyAADF headquarters constructed inside Mount Qasioun, north of Damascus, where the tactical position had to be monitored by multiple operators on several different displays, each of which showed a radar picture of different range. Unsurprisingly, most of the Syrian ground controllers and SAM commanders preferred to operate entirely on their own instead of relying on orders from a headquarters in which there was a permanent state of confusion. Moreover, even once the SA-6s were in position, protected by additional S-75 and S-125 (ASCC/NATO-codename 'SA-3 Goa') SAM systems deployed along the border, and integrated with the help of the Vektor-2ME, the Syrians made the mistake of keeping their anti-aircraft defences in fixed positions. Thus, whether during the 'missile crisis' or once it was over, the Israelis were given plenty of time in which to amass tactical intelligence about them and then develop a plan for their future destruction.[3]

(UN)CONTROLLED ESCALATION

While Philip Habib's mediation failed, it did result in a temporary break in the fighting: an undeclared ceasefire was in force throughout his first and second tour in the Middle East – from 5–12 May. The armistice remained in force until the time Habib eventually convinced Pierre Gemayel to withdraw his surviving troops from Zahle and Begin not to strike Syrian SAM sites, while Assad withdrew his offer of bases to the USSR. Although the Syrians shot down another – the fourth in total – Israeli UAV on 13 May, this time near Damascus, well inside the Syrian airspace,

INFILTRATIONS BY AIR: TAKE 2

More than six months after the first infiltration attempt by air, on 7 March 1981, two gliders – each powered by a 50hp engine – were launched towards Israel, each crewed by one member of the PLF armed with a single AKM assault rifle and several hand-grenades. The first glider landed north of the Israeli border, opposite Rosh HaNikra, and its pilot was quickly captured by the SLA and handed over to the IDF. The second managed to continue its voyage until landing near Kibbutz Afek, about 30km south of the border. Minutes later, the pilot met a young Israeli, who assured him that he was one of the local Arabs and led him towards the Carmel, bypassing all the settlements on the way. Seemingly disoriented, the gunman then asked to be taken to Beirut. Finally, after five hours of walking, the two parted ways, the Israeli rushing to inform the police, who refused to believe him. Meanwhile, the Palestinian entered one of the homes in a nearby settlement and – after stealing some food and water – fell asleep. Upon finding him, the inhabitants called the police and he was arrested.

Following the events of the previous year, the IDF launched preparations to intercept such infiltration attempts, deploying the 947th 'Golan' Battalion equipped with M163 Vulcan air defence artillery systems (essentially, the General Electric M61A1 six-barrel 20mm gun, installed on the M113 APC). A battery of these was deployed on each of four IDF outposts in southern

Lebanon: at Rakefet, Pnina A, Tziporen and Galit. During the night of 16 April, a hot-air balloon of the Thunderbolt 56 type was launched from a site near Dayr Aames, about 20km west of the Israeli border near the Kibbutz Manara – well inside the UNIFIL zone. Around 0300 hours, one of the IDF troops at the Rakefet outpost spotted the huge object moving slowly in the direction of Israel and alerted his platoon leader. Together, they attempted to pinpoint the target, but lost it in the dark early morning sky – until the balloon crew lit the gas burner to climb higher, making themselves visible. Meanwhile, a report about the nocturnal incursion was received by the Tziporen post, about 4km from Rakefet, and the troops there attempted to light up the balloon with the help of illumination shells fired from an 81mm mortar at the coordinates provided by the crew at Rakefet. Eventually, the commander at Tziporen figured out that the targeting data he had received was wrong in azimuth, and started searching in a different direction, eventually sighting a 'moving light'. This area was then lit by a searchlight and illumination shells from 81mm mortars, and the platoon leader of the M163s deployed at Tziporen opened fire. Blinded by the searchlight and flares, the gunner could not use the sights, but was forced to aim on the basis of guidance from his superior. Nevertheless, one of a dozen 10-round bursts hit the target and the balloon crashed to the ground (the M163 at Rakefet had fired some 1,000 rounds about the same time, but failed to strike the balloon). The Israeli artillery then joined the engagement by firing more flare rounds, lighting up the area clearly. Shocked and confused, the crew of the downed balloon were unable to escape: both were caught by the rapid response team of the 931st Battalion, Nahal Infantry Brigade, and gunned down in a short firefight. Their documents identified them as members of Abu Abbas' PLF, armed with one AKM and one M16 assault rifle, and 10 hand-grenades.

Front view of the turret of an M163 Vulcan air defence system: clearly visible are the six-barrel gun and the radar antenna. (IDF)

Begin did not protest. Indeed, by the end of the month, it appeared as if the conflict would be put on hold.

However, Begin – who since the resignation of Ezer Weizmann about a year before had held the posts of both prime minister and minister of defence – then approved a comprehensive offensive into southern Lebanon. Fundamental to this decision was the fact that, while Begin's first cabinet included experienced military officers who often prevented plans for ill-advised military adventures, his second one was dominated by 'hawks', people like Ariel Sharon, Yitzhak Shamir and especially Rafael Eitan – all of

whom saw the military means as the only way of dealing with the Arabs. Indeed, Begin's primary military advisor now became the Chief-of-Staff of the IDF, Eitan, to a degree where Begin trusted Eitan more than Deputy Minister of Defence Mordechai Zipori. Already renowned for his aggressive behaviour towards the Arabs, Eitan became particularly bitter after the death of his son, Yoram, a pilot of the IDF/AF, in an aircraft crash on 4 May 1981. As if this was not enough to endanger the hopes for peace in the region, while – at least nominally – Begin took care of ideology and politics while Eitan dealt with military affairs, in

A French-made M-50 155mm howitzer of the SLA is prepared for firing action. (Albert Grandolini Collection)

reality Begin always tended to make his own decisions, even when this earned him much criticism from his closest subordinates. So it happened that, upon the recommendation of Eitan, on 28 May 1981 – just weeks after the US-mediated ceasefire and only weeks before the next elections in Israel – Begin approved Eitan's request to renew the bombing of PLO bases in southern Lebanon. This new operation was to be conducted following the principle of 'controlled escalation', in the form of a gradually increasing armed conflict, while the public was to be actively distracted by reports about entirely unrelated affairs. As so often before and after, Begin's immediate purpose was of political nature, but the result was an entirely unnecessary escalation into the biggest confrontation in Lebanon since Operation Stone of Wisdom in 1978, and ultimately a war that de-facto is still going on today.[4]

PROVOCATIONS

The IDF/AF also flew an air strike on 28 May against several targets in the Damour area, where a Libyan-supplied SA-9 SAM site had been observed a few weeks earlier. The PLO did not react, as Arafat had promised to refrain from attacks on Israel not only to Habib, but also to the UN Secretary-General, Kurt Waldheim. Nevertheless, the air strikes continued. On 2 June, Israeli jets bombed the Fatah base 11km north of Tyre, and the following night, warships of the IDF/Sea Corps shelled a base of the PFLP on the Bared River, about 13km north of Tripoli. The Palestinians once again did not react, but the IDF/AF strikes went on – although at a lower rate than before – as confirmed by the US Ambassador in Beirut, Robert Dillon: '[T]he PLO refrained from launching military actions against Israel for more than two months, even though the Israelis conducted several air raids during that period. This was a shaky ceasefire, to be sure, but one that nevertheless held, from the Palestinian side.'[5]

What happened next was both ironic and tragic. Considering Begin's outcry about the deployment of the Syrian SAMs, and the fact that the PLO spent most of April and May repairing their damaged bases and restocking their ammunition and supplies, one could have expected the Israelis to target these as a priority. After all, the AMAN knew that the PLO had concluded a major arms deal with Hungary, which resulted in the delivery of a large shipment

via Syria in May. By early June, several dozen T-34/85s and a handful of T-54/55s (increasing the total to about 100) had arrived. The DFLP and PFLP-GC meanwhile received about a dozen BTR-152 APCs each, while their and Fatah's artillery units received two batteries of four BM-21 MRLS rocket launchers each, several M-46 guns, about a dozen 23mm and 57mm anti-aircraft artillery pieces and a second SA-9 SAM site. However, instead of targeting all of these, the Israelis now focused their attention on the Lebanese infrastructure – primarily bridges, roads and minor villages. For example, on 10 July, they bombed militant bases in Dayr el-Zahrani and Nabatiyah, while eight jets stuck at the PFLP-GC's positions near Habbush and A'azze, but the majority of air strikes targeted roads and villages in the Habbush area (north of Nabatiyah), the Zahrani River bridge between Hammoush and Arab-Salim – killing six Lebanese civilians and wounding another 36 – and the area south of Sidon, where at least nine Lebanese civilians were killed and 30 injured. Only now, after six weeks of unprovoked, on/off Israeli air strikes, did the Palestinians decide to hit back: deploying BM-21 MRLS units, the PLO rocketed Qiryat Shemona, killing three.

Surprisingly, the IDF took two days to react to these attacks, as tracking down the PLO's BM-21s apparently proved not as easy as expected. Late in the afternoon of 12 July, a multi-wave air strike bombed the PFLP-GC's positions near the village of Na'ameh – about 2km north of Damour – for 90 minutes. Actually, the small base was seemingly the least of the Israelis' concerns: instead, the pilots demolished a refrigerator factory owned by the Lebanese and numerous adjacent homes, killing seven civilians and wounding 52 more – several because the local populace mistook descending parachute-retarded bombs for downed Israeli pilots. The SyAAF reacted by scrambling a formation of MiG-23MS fighters, but after passing over the Beka'a Valley, these kept their distance. Instead, the Palestinians initiated an artillery duel with Haddad's SLA. The IDF/AF repeated its onslaught on the Lebanese civilians on 14 July when bombing the village of Zifta, outside Sidon, killing 10 and wounding 30, and the Fatah and PFLP-GC positions in Jarmaq and Wadi al-Akhdar, between Damour and Nabatiyah. Moreover, Israeli jets buzzed Beirut at low altitude, breaking the sound barrier and smashing windows in many areas of the city as they went. This time, the SyAAF did try to intervene and four MiG-21MFs streaked low over the Lebanese mountains, attempting to catch one of the A-4s circling over Sidon. They were engaged by four F-16s and lost one MiG. The Palestinians opened fierce anti-aircraft fire and claimed to have hit one of the Israeli jets with their SA-7s, and that this was last seen trailing smoke while fleeing in a southerly direction. In turn, some of the Syrian anti-aircraft positions were hit by Israeli bombs, which caused an explosion of ammunition stored nearby and several large fires. Later the same day, the IDF/AF bombed artillery pieces and BM-

The Zahrani River bridge between Hammoush and Arab-Salim, which was destroyed by Israeli air strikes on 10 July 1981. (IDF)

A Palestinian-operated V-11, twin-barrel 37mm anti-aircraft gun in action against Israeli aircraft in July 1981. (Albert Grandolini Collection)

FIGHTING FALCON VERSUS MiGs

As of early 1981, the Israeli F-16s were still a relatively new factor in the region – to a degree where Babich and his advisors deployed in Syria explained to their allies that they had insufficient information about the recently introduced type. The Fighting Falcon was a somewhat surprising choice of the US Air Force, which, after decades of introducing ever bigger, more complex, heavier and faster interceptors, suddenly opted for a lightweight fighter with the emphasis instead on agility and simple weaponry. While the Soviets knew about the USAF's order for them, and that both major US allies in the Middle East – Iran and Israel – were in rush to follow-up, they still understood very little about the new type's flight characteristics and avionics. At a time when the Soviet air force was introducing to service huge numbers of MiG-23M/MLA/ML/MLDs armed with R-23 and R-24 medium-range air-to-air missiles (ASCC/NATO-codename 'AA-7A/B Apex' and 'AA-7C/D Apex', respectively), military theoreticians of the Soviet General Staff were still having a hard time understanding why their arch-enemy would buy a simple and relatively slow fighter armed only with short-range missiles. With their first MiG-23MF unit still in the process of working up, once again the Syrians selected a MiG-21MF squadron to make the next attempt at challenging the Israeli aerial superiority.[7]

On 14 July 1981, four F-16As from No. 110 'Knights of the North' Squadron were tasked with flying top cover for a formation of A-4s loaded with bombs underway to strike targets in the Sidon area. As usual, the Israeli interceptors took up station off the coast, waiting for the fighter-bombers to complete their task. This time, the four Syrian MiG-21MFs approached at low altitude, flying between the hills: nevertheless, the Israeli C3 system detected them in time to provide ample warning and direct the F-16s to intercept – and to apply ECM that promptly disrupted radio contact between the Syrian formation leader and their ground control. The result was a chaotic situation in which the MiGs lost their way, and one of them was found and shot down by the leader of the Israeli formation (and CO of No. 110 Squadron), Amir Nahumi, using a single AIM-9L Sidewinder. Surviving members of the SyAAF formation returned to Dmeyr, complaining bitterly about the Soviet failure to provide radios that would not be so easy for the Israelis to jam.

21 launchers in the Namariyeh area, about 7km south of Sidon. In all cases, post-strike damage assessment was conducted by UAVs. Nevertheless, the Palestinians hit back with a rocket barrage on Qiryat Shemona, around 2100 hours, which injured 14 people and caused significant damage to several buildings.[6]

TWO WEEKS' WAR

The PLO's retaliation to the attacks of 14 July was almost immediate and the most vicious to that date. Between 0530 and 1830 hours of 15 July, it struck Nahariya and Kiryat Shemona with over 300 rockets and artillery rounds. Three Israelis were killed and nine wounded in Nahariya, and 17 injured in Kryat

Shemona, while both towns suffered considerable damage. The attacks prompted a further escalation by Begin and Eitan – one of which proved beyond disproportional. The following day, the IDF committed not only its air force, but also warships of the Sea Corps and artillery of the Northern Command. Fighter-bombers struck numerous targets in the Damour area, including the headquarters of George Habash's PFLP, artillery positions of Fatah and a building containing the offices of the ALF in Ain el-Hilweh, south of Sidon. However, the primary target was once again the Lebanese infrastructure. Between 1600 and 1800 hours, at least 12 Israeli jets bombed out five bridges over the Litani and Zahrani rivers – including those in Qasmiyeh, Hasbaya and Siniq, el-Zahrani and the one connecting Habbush with Arab-Salim. Another formation bombed the Ayn al-Hilwah refugee camp near

The crew of a PLC-operated M-46 gun remove the tarpaulin that was hiding their weapon from the prying eyes of Israeli pilots (and the cameras of IDF UAVs), before opening fire at northern Israel in July 1981. (Albert Grandolini Collection)

Sidon, and yet another the (US-owned and managed) Medreco oil refinery in Zahrani. Meanwhile, the IDF artillery pounded the Beaufort and Nabatiyah area, while warships shelled Sidon and Tyre. Finally, the 282nd Brigade of the IDF was deployed inside the SLA enclave and near Marjayoun, while the 188th Armoured Brigade and 1st Golani Infantry Brigade were put on alert and ordered to take up positions along the border. All of these moves, and Eitan's statements during a press conference in Tel Aviv, were indications that Israel might be preparing a large attack on the ground. Consequently, the Palestinians put their units on alert and deployed them in defensive positions. Meanwhile, their artillery – bolstered to about 140 rocket launchers and 50 M-46 guns – bombarded not only the SLA's positions, but several settlements in northern Israel too. The artillery of the IDF returned the favour, and by midnight Tyre and even Sidon and Rashidiyeh had been shelled – with tragic consequences, particularly for Lebanese civilians, of whom 28 were killed and more than 60 wounded.

Consequences for the Lebanese and Palestinian civilians from all these actions were terrible: 32 civilians were killed and 97 wounded – fully half of these Lebanese. Predictably, not only were the Lebanese press and public furious at their own government's stance, but that same evening the PLO rocketed several Israeli settlements.

Begin and Eitan remained unimpressed. Working according to the latter's plan from late May, the IDF/AF continued escalating the situation. On the morning of 17 July, it bombed PLO offices in the Fakhani and Tariq al-Jadidah districts near the Shatila refugee camp in Beirut. The bombardment caused massive damage, while numerous bombs equipped with delayed-action fuses went off 45 minutes after impact, as emergency personnel were undertaking rescue work, causing a massacre in which between 100 and 150

people were killed and a further 600 wounded.[8]

GLOVES OFF

Despite the public outcry – at home and abroad – further Israeli air raids followed. On 18 July, the IDF/AF hit the Hamra Bridge north of Sidon and Israeli warships shelled the Medreco refinery outside Zahrani. Air raids were further intensified. The gloves were now off: abandoning all restraint, on 18, 21 and 22 July, the PLO showered northern Israel with rockets with such intensity that six people were killed and 59 injured. Shocked by the onslaught, the local population began to flee towards the south. Within a matter of days, some 40 percent of the population of Qiryat Shemona had left their homes, and there was major disruption of normal life throughout northern Israel. For the first time ever, the Palestinians had achieved something they and numerous other of Israel's enemies had consistently failed to do since 1948. As news of these events spread, a pattern was set for similar operations in the future – not only by the PLO, but by numerous other and much more dangerous militant movements.[9]

Although Israel did not suffer any casualties in the most recent exchanges of fire, it experienced a massive blow to its morale because the civilian population of Upper Galilee had to be evacuated. Unsurprisingly, the Israeli press began severely criticising Begin and his government, whose actions had been unable to silence the Palestinian 'Katyusha rockets'. In turn, Begin now demanded Eitan to 'finish what "he" began', to which Eitan proposed an attack on the Fatah and DFLP headquarters in the so-called Iron Triangle (the area between Fakahani, Sabra and Shatila), in densely populated West Beirut. Both the Chief-of-Staff of the IDF/AF, General David Ivry, and the boss of AMAN, Saguy, were against such an action, but the Israeli prime minister felt otherwise, and the mission was approved.

The morning of 17 July began with reconnaissance aircraft and UAVs ranging deep over Lebanon, while few smaller formations flew mock attacks aimed to pinpoint positions of the Palestine anti-aircraft artillery. Then, at 0700 hours, warships of the IDF/Sea Corps began shelling Rashidiyeh, Ras el-Ain, Sammayeh and Jour el-Nakhl in the Tyre area, and caused heavy damage to the water station in Qasmiyeh. At 0845 hours, the IDF artillery opened fire on Sidon, where one shell landed near a coffee shop, killing four civilians and wounding another 11. At 0930 hours, Israeli fighter-bombers set on fire an oil tank at the Medreco refinery, along with numerous nearby buildings, while warships targeted a bridge on the Zahrani River with missiles. At 1100 hours, the first of three waves of Israeli fighter-bombers attacked multiple targets in West Beirut, including the Fatah headquarters in el-Fakahani, ALF

A grainy but authentic photograph showing an M109 self-propelled howitzer of the IDF in action during the Two Weeks' War. (IDF)

The crew of a PLO-operated MRLS reloading their mount before firing another volley at Upper Galilee. (Albert Grandolini Collection)

attempts at counterbattery fire by hammering the Nabatiyah and Tyre areas.

By this time, the damage caused to the public image of Israel – both domestic and international – was tremendous, to the extent that nothing Begin said about his care to avoid civilian casualties could help any more. An urgent meeting of the Security Council of the UN produced Resolution 490 (1981), which called for the immediate cessation of all armed attacks and reaffirmed the sovereignty, territorial integrity and independence of Lebanon. Nevertheless, the Israelis carried on. On 19 July, the IDF launched its next raid into central southern Lebanon, known as Operation Harpoon, in which a task force from the Parachute Brigade was to demolish a major base of the PFLP-GC outside Msayleh, some 40km from the Israeli border. Inserted with the help of three S-65 helicopters of No. 114 Squadron, the paratroopers split into two large combat teams and a forward controller team. However, the Palestinians were on the alert and the Israelis were spotted upon landing: as a result, the assault force was almost immediately engaged in a fierce firefight. The paras pressed their attack home and overran their objective, but lost one officer killed and seven wounded in

headquarters at Beirut University, DFLP headquarters near the Kuwaiti Embassy and a building used by Fatah near Summerland. At 1145 hours, IDF artillery units shelled Sidon again, this time killing three people and wounding 12 more.

The deadly Israeli strikes reached their high point during the early afternoon. At 1400 hours, 12 fighter-bombers of the IDF/AF bombed Damour and nearby Sa'adiyat, while 15 minutes later, three other formations hit Sidon, Rashidiyeh, el-Bass and Burj el-Shmali. Then at 1430 hours, warships shelled Zahrani and Abu al-Aswad, while about an hour later, the air force bombed Hasbaya, Ain Qenya and other nearby villages. Finally, later that day, the IDF/Sea Corps attempted to block the port of Sidon but was driven away by the artillery of the ALF. After this, there was no holding back for the Palestinians. Early that night, they rocketed and shelled a number of towns and settlements in northern Israel, including Nahariyya and Kiryat Shemona, regardless of IDF

the process. The PFLP-GC lost five militants. Several Bell 212 helicopters were called in to for casualty evacuation, which had to be undertaken under heavy enemy fire. One of the helicopters was damaged and forced to make an emergency landing shortly after crossing back into Israel.[10]

Operation Harpoon was followed by yet more air strikes and artillery barrages. On 19, 20 and 21 July, the IDF/AF, IDF/Sea Corps and the Artillery Corps targeted infrastructure all over southern Lebanon, mainly roads, bridges, electricity installations and factories, primarily along the coast and in the Nabatiyah area. Ten additional bridges were knocked out. Officially at least, the Israelis' aim was to destroy the rate at which the forward Palestinian positions were resupplied: however, the rate at which the militants continued shelling northern Israel did not change much. Thus, while the top brass of the IDF was constantly reporting that the 'terrorists are collapsing', nothing of the kind was actually happening – even though there was no doubt that the Palestinians had been heavily hit, their resistance did not slacken. On 22 July, the Israeli Air Force bombed the bridge at Qasmiyeh while it was undergoing repairs, killing 12 civilians and wounding 14, and once again bombed the Medreco-owned oil refinery in Zahrani, which had no links to the Palestinians. This time, not only were additional fuel tanks set on fire, but the Trans-Arabian Pipeline was also heavily damaged. More air strikes and artillery barrages were reported in the Damour, Sidon and Tyre areas and lasted most of the day, while the Palestinians heavily shelled the SLA-controlled enclave and fired 164 artillery grenades and rockets at Upper Galilee.

Artillery duels continued for several days longer, although both sides opened negotiations for a new ceasefire. Yasser Arafat agreed to the Israeli conditions on 21 July, but the IDF continued shelling even as Begin was discussing the matter with his cabinet. Correspondingly, the Palestinians continued their rocket strikes against northern Israel, where all public life came to a standstill and the IDF had been ordered to assist with damage recovery and provision of basic services – including food and water – to those who remained. It was only at this point that, in the light of growing – and very harsh – criticism of the IDF, Begin and Eitan were forced to admit during a press conference in Metula that the armed forces were unable to fulfil their mission and prevent the shelling of northern Israel. Nevertheless, they refused to stop the onslaught. On 23 July, the IDF/AF bombed bridges at Rashidiyeh, Qasmiyeh, Jarmaq and Hasbaya: during the attack on the latter, the construction collapsed on three civilian cars, killing seven people. The Medreco oil refinery in Zahrani was bombed for the third time and the Trans-Arabian Pipeline set ablaze once again. Warships of the IDF/Sea Corps shelled Sidon and Tyre, while the IDF artillery fired over 500 155mm rounds at other Palestinian positions. The PLO continued shooting back, targeting Kiryat Shemona, Kfar Blum, Misgav Am, Kfar Giladi and Kfar Yehoshua, and – according to UNIFIL – fired a total of 180 shells at the SLA-controlled enclave. Finally, during the night of 23/24 July, commandos of the 13th Flotilla raided a Palestinian base near the power station in Jiyeh, 12km north of Sidon.

A PROTOTYPE WAR

Eventually, a ceasefire negotiated by Philip Habib was agreed for 0130 hours on 24 July 1981. Meanwhile, US President Ronald Reagan openly expressed his displeasure with the Israeli action, blocked further deliveries of F-16s to Israel and de-facto ordered Begin and Eitan to stop the attacks.[11] Nevertheless, in the hours before the deadline, both sides continued their bombardment. The IDF/AF targeted traffic along the coastal road (including at least two civilian cars), while Palestinians fired 30 shells and 40 122mm rockets at the SLA-controlled enclave and northern Israel, to which the IDF and Haddad's forces responded with more than 400 rounds.

The butcher's bill of what the Israelis termed the Two Weeks' War was horrible. According to data subsequently provided by the Lebanese armed forces to the US Embassy in Beirut, 59 percent of those killed (over 500) and 69 percent of the wounded (around 2,000) were Lebanese nationals. Considering that – despite earlier evidence to the contrary – Begin repeatedly turned down US-negotiated ceasefires with the explanation that these 'wouldn't stop PLO raids into northern Israel', it is evident that Israel was actually waging a total war against the land and people of Lebanon, with the aim of not only destabilising but destroying the economy

and the entire country. This can be concluded considering the extent of the damage caused to the local road network, bridges and numerous factories. In turn, Israel reported the loss of six killed and 59 wounded, and significant damage in Nahariya and Qiryat Shemona.

Relatively little is known about military-related statistics: for example, the number of Palestinian and other militants killed in Israeli bombardments remains unknown. Haddad's SLA is known to have spent about 7,500 shells of different calibres. In comparison, the Palestinians fired only about 2,500 artillery and mortar shells, 122mm rockets and 155mm rounds, of which about 1,200 targeted northern Israel. Nevertheless, these were enough to bring life there to a standstill.

The result of this Arab–Israeli conflict was particularly unusual. Technically, it was a stalemate, because neither side lost any territory. However, for the PLO it was a major achievement, for not only did it survive largely intact in the face of immense Israeli military superiority, but its relatively low-technology assets achieved great results. Indeed, Arafat was surprised not only to realise what level of panic his artillery caused in northern Israel – where almost half the population left their homes and all public services and industry fell idle – but also to learn that Israel – and indeed the rock-hard Menachem Begin – had accepted his terms, even if under US pressure. In turn, Israel's inability to halt the rocket attacks was a lesson that not only the PLO was to keep in mind for the future. Indeed, the Two Weeks' War became a prototype for the kind of conflict several other militant organisations were to subsequently fight against Israel.

The truce agreement was interpreted differently by Israel and the PLO. The former claimed that it covered all PLO operations, no matter where, while the latter maintained that it referred exclusively to hostilities across the border between Israel and Lebanon. Predictably, as the Palestinians continued stockpiling weapons in southern Lebanon, the Israelis began complaining and urging that action be taken. In other words, as so often before and after, the ceasefire did not mean peace; it merely froze the conflict as it stood on 24 July 1981. Not only that, but General Ben-Gal of Northern Command said that, 'This ceasefire is just a break … a timely matter, it's not infinite.' Even one of Fatah's commanders concluded: 'Actually, there is a big difference between ceasing fire and ceasing the exchange of shelling between the Joint Forces and the Israeli forces. The ceasing of shelling means a certain thing. Such a decision is usually made in light of certain circumstances and to serve the tactical and strategic position of the Palestinian revolution.'

With hindsight, there is no doubt that both were right: the Arab–Israeli conflict – and thus the Lebanese Civil War – would be resumed before long, and then in the worst imaginable fashion.

EAGLES VERSUS MiGs: TAKE 5

The unprovoked Israeli onslaught on Lebanon grew the appetite for action in both the IDF/AF and the SyAAF, While the Israeli pilots – and their superiors – were looking forward to 'killing more MiGs', the Syrians were keen to, finally, 'hit back in fashion'. Thus, something like a final air battle of this period became an objective for both sides, regardless of the ceasefire. The result was the most controversial air battle of 1981 – or at least one about which the accounts of the two parties are entirely different. In the words of one of the SyAAF officers involved in planning this operation:

> Since 1979, we have launched more than 20 attempts to shoot down one of the Israelis. Without success. Since 1980, the Israelis launched more than 20 attempts to shoot down one of our MiG-25RBs over Lebanon. Without success. Ahmad al-Mehyar, one of our best MiG-25 pilots, had the idea of setting up an ambush for them, using their advantages in our favour.[12]

The plan developed by Mehyar called for a pair of MiG-21MFs to act as bait that would drag F-15s in front of two low-flying MiG-25s, which would then attack simultaneously from opposite sides. It was authorised by Lieutenant General Abazza, and a team of particularly experienced pilots were selected to fly the mission. Early on 29 July, at the T-4 AB, the crews of a squadron equipped with MiG-25RBs were surprised to hear that their mission over Lebanon planned for that day was cancelled. Instead, at the time the sortie was about to be launched, they heard two MiG-25PDs warming up their engines, both fully armed with four R-40 missiles. The two interceptors launched within a few minutes of each other. Once airborne, the first turned north, while the second – flown by Mehyar – continued on a course in the direction of Lebanon. Eventually, the ground control vectored both the MiG-21 and the MiG-25 formations at the same group of targets: a pair of F-15s from No. 133 Squadron and a pair of RF-4Es from No. 119 Squadron underway well to the north of Beirut. What happened next – to both sides – was a result of the MiG-25's high speed.

Because it takes time for radar signals to reach their target and then return to the antenna, the echo to be shown on the display and

While having a potential to match Israeli F-15s, Syrian MiG-25PDs were hampered by the local terrain and superiority of the enemy C3 system. This rare air-to-air photograph shows the first MiG-25PD delivered to Syria: serial number 2400. Notable are the large wing fences containing chaff and flare dispensers, and a dual launcher for R-60M/MK air-to-air missiles under the outboard underwing pylon. (via R. S.)

INTERVIEWS

'Adad' (retired Su-7/20/22 pilot, SyAAF), interview, May 1996.

'Boudros' (retired MiG-21 pilot, SyAAF), interviews, March 2007, October 2008, November 2015, February 2016, April 2018.

'Duha' (retired SyAADF officer), interviews, August 2004, March 2007, July 2013, November 2015, February 2016, April 2018.

'E. R.' (veteran of the IDF), interviews, July 2012.

'Hashim' (retired SyAADF officer), interviews, March 2005, March 2006, July 2013, November 2016.

'Hussam' (retired MiG-21 and MiG-25 pilot, SyAAF), interviews, October 2016, April 2018.

'Ismael' (retired SyAAF MiG-21/Su-22/Su-24 pilot), interview, November 2015.

'Jabbar' (retired officer of the Syrian Military Intelligence), interviews, June 2003, March 2006.

'Mouhannad' (MiG-21 and Su-22 pilot, SyAAF), interviews, August 2004, June 2011, July 2013, December 2016, April 2018.

'Nabil' (SA-6/11/17 operator, SyAADF), interviews, April 2001, March 2007, October 2007, July 2013, November 2016.

'Talal' (CO SAM-brigade, SyAAF/SyAADF), interviews, April 2001, August 2004, March 2005, March 2006, March 2007, October 2007, October 2008, December 2012, July 2013, November 2015, December 2016, April 2018.

the controller to react – with this taking, depending on the range to the target, between 15 and 30 seconds – both sides reacted much too slowly and the Syrian plot fell apart. Instead of the Israelis first detecting the two MiG-21s and engaging them, the northern MiG-25 approached the targets before this happened. The Syrian ground control ordered it to attack, but the Israelis meanwhile descended, making it impossible for the MiG-25 pilot to open fire. In turn, although the Israeli ground control should have detected the MiG while this was still about 40 miles (64.5km) north of the Eagles, the Syrian came in at a speed of 950 knots (1,760km/h). As result, the MiG-25 was only about 6 miles (9.7km) away when the lead F-15, piloted by Saul Simon, fired a single AIM-7F missile, which streaked upwards and impacted on the underside of the Syrian jet, causing it to crash. Only at that point had the Israelis detected the MiG-21 pair that was planned to act as bait. Indeed, the two Syrians performed as planned and turned east, pulling the two Eagles with them. It was then that Mehyar, still underway at low altitude, approached to within about 20 miles (32km) before powering up his Smerch-2A and ripple-firing two R-40RDs. The Israeli fighters were forced into evasive manoeuvring, and both the R-40s missed. By the time the F-15s were ready to counterattack, Mehyar had

already completed a near 180-degrees turn and blazed away in an easterly direction. Both Simon and his wingman, Amir Greenfeld, fired one AIM-7F, but one missile detonated about 500 metres behind the target while the other failed to lock on to its target. With additional MiGs approaching the combat zone, which was now less than 10 miles (16km) from Syria, the Israeli ground control ordered both of its fighters to disengage.

As far as the Israeli versions goes, this was the closest the Syrians had come to shooting down an F-15 – and even then, they achieved nothing while losing another of their brand-new MiG-25PDs. For the Syrians, however, there was – and there remains – no doubt that Mehyar here became their first pilot to defeat an Israeli F-15.

Three Syrian MiG-25 pilots with one of their mounts at T-4 AB. Note that in the background, installed under the wing of the jet, are one R-40TD (left) and one R-40 (right) air-to-air missile. (via Albert Grandolini)

BIBLIOGRAPHY

Andersson, M.S., *Leaving them to stew in their own Juice: US–Syrian Relations and the Lebanese Civil War, 1981–1984* (Oslo: University of Oslo, 2018)

Andrew, C.M., *France Overseas: The Great War and the Climax of French Imperial Expansion* (London: Thames and Hudson, 1981)

Asher, D., *The Egyptian Strategy for the Yom Kippur War: An Analysis* (McFarland & Co. Inc., 2009)

Asher, D., 'The Syrian Invasion of Lebanon: Military Moves as a Political Tool', *Ma'arachot* (in Hebrew) (June 1977)

Avi-Ran, R., 'The Syrian Involvement in Lebanon since 1975', in *Studies in International Politics, the Leonard Davis Institute for International Relations, the Hebrew University of Jerusalem* (Boulder, CO: Westview Press, 1991)

Babich, (Col.) V.K., *Interceptors Change Tactics* (Moscow: 1983) (in Russian)

Babich, (Col.) V.K., 'MiG-21 vs Mirage III', *Aviation and Time* (in Russian)

Babich, (Col.) V.K., 'MiG-23 Fighters in Lebanon War', *Aviation and Time* (in Russian)

Badran, T., 'Lebanon's Militia Wars', *The Middle East Review of International Affairs*, posted online at the Foundation for Defense of Democracies, fdd.org (8 July 2008)

Baker, R., *King Husain and the Kingdom of Hejaz* (Cambridge: The Oleander Press, 1979)

Barr, J., *A Line in the Sand: Britain, France and the Struggle that Shaped the Middle East* (London: Simon & Schuster UK Ltd, 2011)

Benjamin, M., *Drone Warfare: Killing by Remote Control* (New York: OR Books, 2012)

Brower, K., 'The Israel Defence Forces, 1948–2017', *Mideast Security and Policy Studies No. 150* (Ramat Gan, Israel: The Begin–Sadat Centre for Strategic Studies, Bar-Ilan University, 2018)

Brynen, R., *Sanctuary and Survival: The PLO in Lebanon* (Boulder, CO: Westview Press, 1990)

Centre for Military Studies, *The History of the Syrian Army* (in Arabic) (Damascus: Centre for Military Studies, 2001–02)

Chennel, B., LIebert, M. & Moreau, E., *Mirage III/5/50 en service à l'étranger* (Paris: LELA Presse, 2014)

Clarke, G.M., *The 1982 Israeli War in Lebanon: Implications for Modern Conventional Warfare* (Washington: The National War College, 1983)

Clary, D.E., *The Bekaa Valley – A Case Study* (Alabama: Air Command and Staff College, 1988)

Clovis, Ch., *First Confrontations: 100-Day War, Volume 1* (Beirut: self-published, 2009)

Clovis, Ch., *The Battles of Syria in Lebanon, Volume 2* (Beirut: self-published, 2010)

Cobban, H., *The Palestinian Liberation Organisation: People, Power, and Politics* (Cambridge: Cambridge University Press, 2008)

Cooper, T., *MiG-23 Flogger in the Middle East: Mikoyan I Gurevich MiG-23 in Service in Algeria, Egypt, Iraq, Libya and Syria, 1973–2018* (Warwick: Helion & Co, 2018)

Cooper, T., *Syrian Conflagration: The Civil War, 2011–2013* (Solihull: Helion & Co, 2015)

Cooper, T., Grandolini, A. & Delalande, A., *Libyan Air Wars, Part 1* (Solihull: Helion & Co Ltd, 2014)

Cooper, T., Grandolini, A. & Delalande, A., *Libyan Air Wars, Part 2* (Solihull: Helion & Co Ltd, 2016)

Cooper, T., Grandolini, A. & Delalande, A., *Libyan Air Wars, Part 3* (Solihull: Helion & Co Ltd, 2016)

Cooper, T. & Salti, P., *Hawker Hunters at War: Iraq and Jordan, 1958–1967* (Solihull: Helion & Co, 2016)

Dahl, B., *The Lebanese-Palestinian Conflict in 1973: The Social (De)Construction of Lebanese Sovereignty* (Oxford: University of Oxford, Faculty of Oriental Studies, 2006; Thesis)

Dawisha, A.I., 'Syria in Lebanon: Assad's Vietnam?', *Foreign Policy No. 33* (Winter 1978–79)

Dupuy, Col. T.N. & Blanchard, W., *The Almanac of World Military Power* (New York: T.N. Dupuy Associates, 1972)

Eldar, M., *Flotilla 11: The Battle for Citation* (in Hebrew) (Tel Aviv: Ma'ariv Book Guild, 1996)

Eldar, M., *Flotilla 13: The Story of Israel's Naval Commando* (in Hebrew) (Tel Aviv: Ma'ariv Book Guild, 1993)

Esber, F., 'The United States and the 1981 Lebanese Missile Crisis', *Middle East Journal*, Vol. 70, No. 3 (Summer 2016)

Flintham, V., *Air Wars and Aircraft: A Detailed Record of Air Combat 1945 to the Present* (London: Arms and Armour Press, 1989)

Frenkel, M. & Hirsh, A., *Ground Raid: Its part in Strategy and Building the Force* (private document)

Givati, M., *The Steel was Forged in their Hands* (in Hebrew) (Tel Aviv: Ministry of Defence Publishing, 1998)

Green, S., *Living by the Sword: America and Israel in the Middle East* (Brattleboro, VT: Amana Books, 1988)

Gunston, B., *An Illustrated Guide to Modern Fighters and Attack Aircraft* (London: Salamander Books Ltd, 1980)

Halperin, M., *Nocturnal Predators: The Story of Golani's Reconnaissance Unit* (in Hebrew) (Tel Aviv: Yedioth Ahronoth Publishing, 2018)

Huthes, M., 'The Banality and Brutality: British Armed Forces and the Repression of the Arab Revolt in Palestine, 1936–1939', *English Historical Review*, Vol. CXXIV, No. 507 (April 2009)

Ilyin, V., 'MiG-23 in the Middle East', *Aviation and Time* (in Russian)

Ilyin, V., 'MiG-23: Long Path to Perfection', *Aviation and Time* (in Russian)

International Center for Transnational Justice (ICTJ), *Lebanon's Legacy of Political Violence: A Mapping of Serious Violations of International Human Rights and Humanitarian Law in Lebanon, 1975–2008* (September 2013)

Israeli Ministry of Foreign Affairs, *Israel's Foreign Relations, Volume 7: 1981–1982* (Israeli Ministry of Foreign Affairs/mfa.gov.il/MFA/ForeignPolicy/MFADocuments)

Israeli State Archive, *South Lebanon, Part A: July 1981* (in Hebrew) (Israeli State Archive, 000357a, 2017)

Jacobs, B.M., *Operation Peace for Galilee; Operational Brilliance, Strategic Failure* (Newport, RI: Naval War College, 1995)

Jawaid, I., *Lebanon in the Israeli Security Perspective* (PhD thesis, Jawaharlal Nehru University, 1990; available via *shdohganga.inflibnet.ac.in* as file No. 15101)

Jelavic, T., *No. 352 (Y) R.A.F. Squadron* (Zagreb: Multigraf d.o.o., 2003)

Jureidini, Paul A., McLurin, R.D. & Price, James M., 'Military Operations in Selected Lebanese Built-up Areas, 1975–1978', *Technical Memorandum 11-79* (Maryland: US Army Engineering Laboratory, 1984)

Kassis, S., *30 Years of Military Vehicles in Lebanon* (Beirut: Elite Group, 2003)

Kemp, G.F., *Lebanon, June–July (1 & 2)* (Ronald Reagan Presidential Library)

Kessing's Record of World Events, Volume 27: June 1981, Lebanon (Cleveland: Keesing's Worldwide LLLC, 1981)

Kordoba, Y., 'From Missile Crisis to War' (in Hebrew), *Ma'arachot* magazine, Vol. 285 (December 2002)

Lawson, F.H., 'Syria's Intervention in the Lebanese Civil War, 1976: A Domestic Conflict Explanation', *International Organization*, Vol. 38 (Summer 1984) (The MIT Press)

Konzelmann, G., *Damaskus: Oase Zwischen Hass und Hoffnung* (Frankfurt/Main: Ullstein Buch, 1996)

Kotlobovskiy, A.B., *MiG-21 in Local Wars* (Kiev: ArchivPress, 1997) (in Russian)

Lake, J. & Donald, D. (eds), *McDonnell F-4 Phantom: Spirit in the Skies, Updated and Expanded Edition* (Norwalk, CT: AIRtime Publishing Inc.,1992)

Lebanese Forces Official Website, 'Veteran Memories from 100-Days-War', Lebanese-forcecs.com (2020)

Maisel, Brig. Gen. E.D., 'Transition Period: The Aid Project for the Residents of Southern Lebanon', *IDF Magazine* (in Hebrew) (January 2014)

Mandel, R., 'Israel in 1982: The War in Lebanon', *Jewish American Yearbook* (1984)

Manos, Brigadier General O., 'The War of Artillery Commander of Northern Command' (in Hebrew), IDF Artillery Heritage Website, www.beithatothan.org.il (2013)

Marchenko, A., 'Syrian Mission', *Express Novosti*, Vol. 39 (319) (26 September – 2 October 2003) (in Russian)

McLaurin, R.D., 'The Battle of Zahle', *Technical Memorandum 8-86* (Maryland: US Army Human Engineering Laboratory, 1986)

Menargues, A., *Les secrets de la guerre Du Liban: du coup d'Etat de Bachir Gemayel aux Massacres des Camps Palestiniens* (Paris: Albin Michel, 2004)

Meyer, K.E. & Brysac, S.B., *Kingmakers: The Invention of the Modern Middle East* (New York: W.W. Norton & Co., 2009)

Michel, M.L., *Clashes: Air Combat over North Vietnam, 1965–1972* (Annapolis, MD: Naval Institute Press, 1997)

Mladenov, A., 'MiG-23MLD vs Western Fighters: The Soviet Air Force View', *Air Forces Monthly* (October 2003)

Mollo, A., *The Armed Forces of World War II* (New York: Crown Publishing, 1981)

Morris, B., *Righteous Victims: A History of the Zionist-Arab Conflict, 1881–1999* (London: John Murray, 1999)

Morris, B., *The Birth of the Palestinian Refugee Problem, 1947–1949* (Cambridge: Cambridge Middle East Library, 2004)

Moukiiad, Major General M.A., *My Life* (in Arabic) (Damascus: az-Zakhira, 2005)

Naour, D., *Did all Roads really lead to Beirut? Menachem Begin's Lebanese Policy, 1977–1982* (Ariel, Israel: Ariel University, 2020)

Nisan, M., *The Conscience of Lebanon: A political Biography of Etienne Sakr (Abu-Arz)* (London: Frank Cass Publishers, 2003)

Norton, B., *75 Years of the Israeli Air Force, Volume 1: The First Quarter Century, 1948–1973* (Warwick: Helion & Company Ltd, 2020)

Norton, B., *75 Years of the Israeli Air Force, Volume 2: The Last Half Century, 1973–2023* (Warwick: Helion & Company Ltd, 2021)

Norton, B., *75 Years of the Israeli Air Force, Volume 3: Training, Combat Support, Special Operations, Naval Operations and Air Defense, 1948–2023* (Warwick: Helion & Company Ltd, 2021)

O'Ballance, E., *Civil War in Lebanon, 1975–92* (London: Palgrave Macmillan, 1998)

'Operation Harpoon', Website of the Parachute Brigade Reconnaissance Unit, archive.li/3bu6H

Rahav, Brigadier General E. & Yehoshua, Colonel, 'My Participation in Operation High Voltage, April 1980', *Maritime Heritage Watch*, moreshetyamit.net (2020) (in Hebrew)

Raspletin, Dr A.A., 'History PVO' (website in Russian: historykpvo.narod2.ru) (2013)

Richardson, D., *Modern Fighting Aircraft: F-16 Fighting Falcon* (London: Salamander Books, 1983)

Sakal, General E., *Lebanon Days: 252 Division in Operation Peace for Galilee* (Tel Aviv: 2019)

Sayigh, Y., 'Palestinian Military Performance in the 1982 War', *Journal of Palestine Studies*, Vol. 12, No. 4 (Summer 1983), pp.3–24

Schiff, Z. & Ya'ari, E., *Israel's Lebanon War* (New York: Simon and Schuster, 1984)

Shachar, A., *History of Ordnance Corps, 1967–1985* (in Hebrew) (Tel Aviv: Himush Publishing, 2006)

Shukairy, A., *The Great Defeat; Major Defeat of Kings and Presidents* (Cairo: Arab Foundation for Publishing and Distribution, 2005)

Shur, A. & Halevi, A., *Sayeret Matkal: The Greatest Operations of the Unit* (in Hebrew) (Rishon le Tsion: Yediot Books Publishing, 2020)

SIPRI, *World Armament and Disarmament/SIPRI Yearbook 1981* (London: Taylor & Francis Ltd, 1981)

Solley, G.C., *The Israeli Experience in Lebanon, 1982–1985* (Quantico: Marine Corps Command and Staff College, 1987)

Tereshenko, N.M., 'Mission in Damascus', *Military History Magazine* 12 (1990)

Thomas, W. E., *Operation Peace for Galilee: An Operational Analysis with Relevance Today* (Newport, RI: Naval War College, 1998)

Thompson, Sir R. (ed.), *War in Peace: An Analysis of Warfare since 1945* (London: Orbis Publishing, 1981)

'Unit 504: Presentation of Operation Menora: Attacking Terrorist Bases in Ramat Arnon (Beaufort Area)' (in Hebrew), Website of Veterans of the Unit 504, sfilev2.f-static.com

United Nations, *United Nations Charter, Chapter XV, Article 98, Supplement No. 6 (1979–1984), Volume 6* (Repertory of Practice of United Nation Organs, legal.un.org)

United Nations, *Report of the Secretary-General of the United Nations: Interim Force in Lebanon (for the period from 16 June to 10 December 1981)* (New York: United Nations Digital Library, 1981)

Van Creveld, M., *The Sword and the Olive* (New York: BBS Public Affairs, 1998)

Weinberger, N.J., *Syrian Intervention in Lebanon: The 1975–1976 Civil War* (New York: Oxford University Press, 1986)

Ya'akov, Z. & Sagi, S-T., *Artillery Corps in Operation Peace for Galilee* (in Hebrew) (Kinneret: Zmora-Bitan Publishing House Ltd., 2015)

Zonder, M., *The Elite Unit of Israel* (in Hebrew) (Jerusalem: Keter Publishing House Ltd, 2000)

Various issues of the *IAF Magazine*, *Davar* newspaper (1979, 1980, 1981), *Ma'riv* newspaper (1979, 1980, 1981)

NOTES

Chapter 1

1 Unless stated otherwise, based on Schiff *et al.*, pp.11–25; Badran, 'Lebanon's Militia Wars'; Kassis, *Military Vehicles*; & Sayigh, 'Palestinian Military Performance in the 1982 War', pp.7–8.

2 Unless stated otherwise, based on Badran, 'Lebanon's Militia Wars'; Kassis, *Military Vehicles*. For details on the ALA, see Volume 1, pp.51, 61, 64.

3 Unless stated otherwise, based on Gabriel, *Operation Peace for Galilee*, pp.44–46, & Sayigh, 'Palestinian Military Performance in the 1982 War', pp.7–8.

4 Col. T.N. Dupuy, & W. Blanchard, *The Almanac of World Military Power* (New York: T.N. Dupuy Associates, 1972).

5 Unless stated otherwise, based on McLaurin, 'The Battle of Zahle', & International Center for Transitional Justice, *Lebanon's Legacy of Political Violence: A Mapping of Serious Violations of International Human Rights and Humanitarian Law in Lebanon, 1976–2008* (September 2013) (henceforth ICTJ-Report), pp.20–25.

6 ICTJ-Report, p.25, & Jawaid, pp.193–194.

Chapter 2

1 Unless stated otherwise, based on O'Ballance, *Civil War in Lebanon*; Choueifaty, *First Confrontations*; Jureidini *et al.*, *Military Operations in Selected Lebanese Built-up Areas*; Nisan, *The Conscience of Lebanon*; veteran recollections from the Hundred Days' War posted on the official website of the Lebanese Armed Forces (Lebanese-forces.com); and contemporary press reports.

2 Unless stated otherwise, based on ICTJ-Report, pp.25–26; Schiff *et al.*, *Lebanon War*; O'Ballance, *Civil War in Lebanon*; Choueifaty, *First Confrontations*; Jureidini *et al.*, *Military Operations in Selected Lebanese Built-up Areas*; Nisan, *The Conscience of Lebanon*; veteran recollections from the Hundred Days' War posted on the official website of the Lebanese Forces (Lebanese-forces.com); and contemporary press reports (for example: *Reuters*, 'Israel Tightens Security along its border in Lebanon as Fighting continues in Beirut', 7 July 1978, & *Reuters*, 'Beirut Christian District of Ain Rummaneh comes under Fire again', 29 August 1978).

3 'Near East/North Africa Report', *Foreign Broadcast Information Service* (henceforth FBIS) (22 March 1982), p.22.

4 Unless stated otherwise, based on ICTJ-Report, pp.25–26; Schiff *et al.*, *Lebanon War*, pp.24–26; O'Ballance, *Civil War in Lebanon*; Choueifaty, *First Confrontations*; Jureidini *et al.*, *Military Operations in Selected Lebanese Built-up Areas*; Nisan, *The Conscience of Lebanon*; veteran recollections from the Hundred Days' War posted on the official website of the Lebanese Forces (Lebanese-forces.com); and contemporary press reports.

5 Unless stated otherwise, based on ICTJ-Report, pp.25–26, & Schiff *et al.*, *Lebanon War*, pp.26–27.

Chapter 3

1 Unless stated otherwise, based on Givati, *The Steel was forged in their Hands*; Barzilai, 'Chariots of Fire', *Haaretz* (11 September

2002); Shachar, *History of Ordnance Corps*; Sakal, *Lebanon Days*; Brower, *The Israel Defence Forces*; and reporting in the daily *Davar* (in Hebrew).

2 Unless stated otherwise, based on Ya'akov *et al.*, *Artillery Corps in Operation Peace for Galilee*.

3 Unless stated otherwise, based on Norton, *75 Years of Israeli Air Force*, Vol. 2, pp.5–16, & Richardson, *F-16*, pp.3–6.

4 Norton, *75 Years of the Israeli Air Force*, Vol. 2, pp.14–15.

5 Unless stated otherwise, the following two sub-chapters are based on Ben Galim, *IDF/Sea Corps magazine*, Vol. 182, January 1991; reports in the daily newspaper *Davar*; 'Sa'ar-4.5 (Hetz) Class Fast Attack Craft of the Israeli Navy', Naval Analyses website, www.navalanalyses.com; Almog, 'Israel's Naval Force: An Essential Tier for Decision on the Battlefield'; Army and Strategy (May 2011); & Norton, *75 Years of the Israeli Air Force*, Vol. 3, pp.26–27.

6 During the second half of the 1970s, the IDF/Sea Corps also ran testing of US-made Flagstaff-2-class hydrofoils, armed with US-made BGM-84A Harpoon and Israeli-made Gabriel Mk 3 anti-ship missiles. Run as Project Zivanit, this effort was strongly promoted by the Chief-of-Staff, IDF/Sea Corps, Michael Barkai. In 1978, it resulted in a contract for the US corporation Grumman to construct the first two vessels and prepare materials for a further 18. However, Barkai had been relieved of his command in 1979, and both Eitan and Weizman strongly opposed this project. Eventually, both ships were launched, but the contract was then cancelled.

7 Starting in 1969, Israel acquired a mix of 38 Sikorsky S-65C-2/3s and about a dozen CH-53A airframes, some directly from the manufacturer, others from surplus stocks of the US Marine Corps. Additional 12-14 CH-53s, and two former Austrian Air Force S-65Ös were acquired after 1991.

8 Eldar, *Flotilla 11*; Maiser, 'Transition Period', *Davar* (multiple volumes from 1977–78); *Reuters*, 'Lebanon: Palestinian and Leftist Forces Display captured Arms and dead Rightist Troops in captured Village' (4 March 1978). Notably, regardless of many reports of the contrary, the IDF never handed over any of the M51 Shermans armed with 105mm gun to the Lebanese Christians. Indeed, it never delivered Tirans with such guns either and only vehicles with 100mm guns were supplied.

Chapter 4

1 'Jabbar', interviews, 06/2003 & 03/2006.

2 'Jabbar', interview, 06/2003.

3 Nordeen, p.163; Adad, interview, 05/1996; Jabbar, interviews, 06/2003 & 03/2006.

4 For details, see Vol. 1, pp.64–66.

5 'Jabbar', interviews, 06/2003 & 03/2006.

6 Unless stated otherwise, this sub-chapter is based on 'Adad', interview, 05/1996; Jabbar, interviews, 06/2003 & 03/2006.

7 According to Jabbar, subsequent investigations with the help of Soviet advisors revealed that due to the long flight at speeds above Mach 1.5, all four R-3S missiles were overheated and thus rendered non-operational. The reason was that as of this time, SyAAF MiG-23MS aircraft were still armed in the configuration in which they were delivered: with four R-3S missiles (in addition to their twin-barrel, internally installed GSh-23-2 23mm cannon). It was only after this incident that the Syrians did the same as the Iraqis had already been doing: rewiring their MiG-23MSs for more advanced – and heat-resistant – R-13M (ASCC/NATO-codename 'AA-2C Advanced Atoll') air-to-air missiles, the seeker-heads of which were cooled with the help of liquid nitrogen from a bottle installed in the launch rail. As far as is known, this was to become the last air combat involving Hijazi: for medical reasons, he was subsequently taken off flying supersonic jets, changed to Syrian Air and flew Tupolev Tu-154 airliners for the rest of his career.

8 Unless stated otherwise, content of this box is based on 'Jabbar', interview, 06/2003; Cohen, pp.440–443; and correspondence with Iftach Spector & Bill Norton, 2020–21.

9 Moukiiad, *My Life*, Chapter 6. With Israeli descriptions of this aerial combat being widely published since 1979, this account is based on recollections by Syrian sources. The principal difference to what the IDF/AF claimed is that the Israelis say

that all of their AIM-7Fs fired at the start of this engagement had missed their targets; and that the first kill was scored by a Python-3, the second by an AIM-7F and the other three by AIM-9Gs and guns.

10 Abazza was a highly decorated veteran of wars with Israel from 1967–73, and was appointed Chief-of-Staff SyAAF, on 1 July 1978.

11 Unless stated otherwise, content of this box is based on 'Jabbar', interivew, 06/2003; Cohen, pp.440–443; and correspondence with Iftach Spector & Bill Norton, 2020–021.

12 'Jabbar', interviews, 06/2003 & 03/2006; 'Boudros', interview, 03/2007. Notably, the Israelis credited their pilots with four MiG-21s in this aerial combat, which was – 'unofficially' – confirmed by Moukiiad in *My Life*, Chapter 6. However, 'Jabbar' and 'Boudros' have – independently from each other – recalled that three MiG-21s were shot down, while the fourth managed an emergency landing at Ryak AB.

13 'Jabbar', interview, 03/2006; Moukiiad, Chapter 6; & Konzelmann, pp.334–336. Arguably, as of 1981, the Soviets would have had very little in terms of advanced aircraft to offer: with types like the MiG-29 and Su-27 still undergoing development and being years away from entering series production and operational service, their best tactical fighter-interceptor of the time was the MiG-23MLA/ML. While an order of magnitude better than the almost useless MiG-23MS, delivered to the SyAAF in 1974, and even MiG-23MFs that were still in the process of entering service in Syria, even these eventually turned out to be no match for F-15s and F-16s.

14 'Jabbar', interviews, 06/2003 & 03/2006.

15 Green, *Living by the Sword*, p.155.

Chapter 5

1 'The Massacre of the Military Artillery School at Aleppo – Special Report', The Syrian Human Rights Committee (3 November 2003).

2 The operation at Kibbutz Misgav Am received much praise in the public and was declared a major success of Sayeret Matkal – for which it was important to recover its self-confidence after a painful failure during the Ma'a lot hostage crisis of 1974: on the contrary, the involvement of the Golani Brigade was entirely ignored for years after. Moreover, away from all the euphoria, the subsequent investigation pointed out numerous issues. The first of these was that a team of five not only penetrated the Israeli border unobserved, but also passed a minefield and cut through the electric fence on the other side. Eventually, it turned out that the minefield had been rendered non-operational and the electronic fence damaged by a bush fire several months earlier, and neither was ever repaired. Furthermore, the first assault attempt by the Golani Brigade was concluded to be entirely pointless: the situation had been developing for only two hours, and there was no need to rush and endanger the hostages. Finally, the commander of Unit 269, and the new Chief of AMAN, General Yehoshua Saguy, found it pointless for Unit 269 to be deployed for hostage-rescue operations inside Israel. The task of crisis-management in such situations was henceforth passed to the Israeli police and its Counter-Terrorism Unit (Yamam).

3 The following sub-chapter is based on Shur *et al.*, *Sayeret Matkal*; Zonder, *The Elite Unit of Irael*; Halperin, *Nocturnal Predators*; Eldar, *Flotilla 13*; and Rahav *et al.*, 'My Participation in Operation High Voltage'.

4 The Sikorsky S-65C-3 is the commercial variant of this heavy-lift helicopter, better known under its military designation CH-53D Sea Stallion. In Israel, the type is known under the designation Yas'ur. By the late 1970s, about two dozen were operated by Nos 114 and 118 Squadrons, IDF/AF.

5 Unless stated otherwise, this and the following sub-chapters are based on Brigadier General Ori Manos, 'The War of Artillery Commander of Northern Command', IDF Artillery Heritage website, beithatotahn.org.il; O'Ballance, *Civil War in Lebanon*; Frenkel *et al.*, 'Ground Raid'; *IAF Magazine*, Vol. 125 (1 October 2000); *Davar*, different issues from 1979, 1980 and 1981 (all in Hebrew), *Ma'ariv*, different issues from 1980; 'Mayor of Jerusalem, Nir Barkat: Story of Operation Movil' (in Hebrew), Youtube.com (2011); 'Unit 504: Presentation of Operation

Menora; Attacking Terrorist Bases in Ramat Arnon (Beaufort Area)' (in Hebrew), website of Veterans of Unit 504, sfilev2.f-static.com; Yosef Nisimov, '41 Years Ago: Operation deep inside Lebanon that Benni Gantz took part in' (TV-documentary in Hebrew), *Channel 20* (2021).

6 Interviews with former Syrian military officers (see Bibliography) & CIA, 'Syria's Elite Military Units: Key to Stability and Succession: An Intelligence Assessment', NESA 87-10012 (February 1987), CIA FOIA Electronic Reading Room (henceforth CIA/FOIA/ERR); V.A. Dudchenko, 'Commentary to "Syrian Sketches" by O. Akopov', *Artofwar* magazine (25 April 2007) (in Russian); V.A. Dudchenko, 'Persona non grata', *Artofwar* (17 March 2009) (in Russian); & Cooper, *Syrian Conflagration*, p.9.

7 Unless stated otherwise, this chapter is based on O'Ballance, *Civil War in Lebanon*; McLaurin, 'The Battle of Zahle'; Clovis, *The Battles of Syria in Lebanon, Volume 2*; Menargues, *Les secrets de la guerre au Liban*; & veteran recollections on the official website of the Lebanese Armed Forces (Lebanese-forces.com).

8 A.N. Pochtarjov, 'On the Lebanese Track', *Red Star* (28 February 2002); Konzelmann, pp.331–335; & Markovskiy, 'Hot June 1982'.

9 Unless stated otherwise, content of this box is based on 'Jabbar', interivew, 06/2003; & correspondence with Iftach Spector & Bill Norton, 2020–21.

Chapter 6

1 Unless stated otherwise, this chapter is based on O'Ballance, *Civil War in Lebanon*; Schiff *et al.*, *Lebanon War*; McLaurin, 'The Battle of Zahle'; Clovis, *The Battles of Syria in Lebanon, Volume 2*; Menargues, *Les secrets de la guerre au Liban*; & veteran recollections posted on the official website of the Lebanese Armed Forces (Lebanese-forces.com).

2 Unless stated otherwise, content of this box is based on 'Jabbar', interivew, 06/2003; correspondence with Iftach Spector & Bill Norton, 2020–21; Ilyin, 'MiG-23 in the Middle East'; & 'We were not only Advisors: we have fought Wars in Syria', *survincity.com* (1 March 2013). In 1983, V.K. Babich – decorated a Hero of the Soviet Union in the 1970s – gained some prominence in the West by publishing the book *Interceptors Change Tactics*, in which he discussed latest developments in aerial warfare.

3 Eldar, *Flotilla 11*; Maiser, 'Transition Period', *Davar* (multiple volumes from 1981).

4 Unless stated otherwise, based on Green, *Living by the Sword*, p.155; Brigadier General Ori Manos, 'The War of Artillery Commander of Northern Command', IDF Artillery Heritage website, beithatotahn.org.il; O'Ballance, *Civil War in Lebanon*; Frenkel *et al.*, 'Ground Raid'; *IAF Magazine*, Vol. 135 (1 October 2000); *Davar*, different issues from 1979, 1980 and 1981 (all in Hebrew), *Ma'ariv*, different issues from 1980; Yosef Nisimov, '41 Years Ago: Operation deep inside Lebanon that Benni Gantz took part in' (TV-documentary in Hebrew), *Channel 20* (2021).

5 'Jabbar', interview, 03/2006; Flintham, *Air Wars And Aircraft*, p.68; & Ilyin, 'MiG-23 in the Middle East'. Notably, on the same day (26 April 1981), the SyAAF lost a MiG-23UB underway on a mission of visual reconnaissance south of Beirut: the jet was shot down by the Palestinians, using an SA-7 MANPAD.

6 Schiff *et al.*, p.34.

7 Green, *Living by the Sword*, p.156, & Schiff *et al.*, pp.34–35.

Chapter 7

1 Unless stated otherwise, this chapter is based on *Israel's Foreign Relations*, Vol. 7; Schiff *et al.*, *Israel's Lebanon War*; Esber, 'The United States and the 1981 Lebanese Missile Crisis'; *United Nations Charter*, Chapter XV, Article 98; Schiff *et al.*, pp.35–37; R. Brynen, *Sanctuary and Survival*; Benjamin, *Drone Warfare*; *Davar* (in Hebrew), multiple volumes from 1981; *Red Star* (in Russian), multiple volumes from 1981–82; Israeli Ministry of Foreign Affairs, *Israel's Foreign Relations*, Vol. 7 (1981–82); Israeli State Archive, *South Lebanon, Part A* (July 1981); Naor, *Did all Roads really lead to Beirut?*; Andersson, *Leaving them to Stew in their own Juice*; Cordoba, 'From Missile Crisis to War'; Kemp, *Lebanon June–July* (1 and 2); Secretary-General of the United Nations, *Interim Force in Lebanon*.

2 G.P. Yashkin, 'We fought in Syria', *VKO* (April 1988).

3 Description of the SyAADF's IADS deployed in Lebanon of 1981 as provided by 'Duha', 'Hashim' and 'Nabil. Another of the interviewed Syrian officers, and one of the interviewed Algerian officers briefed about Syrian experiences from Lebanon in 1981–82, have described the resulting 'integration' as 'ridiculous'. Independently from each other, they both observed that this resulted in the information being provided on three or four different scopes, each of which was presenting the data in different format. In action, many Syrian officers thus preferred acting on their own rather than depending on the centralised IADS and waiting for commands from above. According to G.P. Yashkin, in 'We fought in Syria', *VKO* (April, 1988), Syrian SAM units deployed inside Lebanon shot down 'three F-16s and one F-15 within days of their arrival'.

4 Schiff *et al.*, p.25.

5 Green, *Living by the Sword*, pp.156–158.

6 Green, *Living by the Sword*, p.160.

7 'Boudros', interviews, 03/2007 & 10/2008; 'Hussam', interview, 10/2016; 'Jabbar', interviews, 06/2003 & 03/2006; 'Mouhannad', interview, 08/2004.

8 Green, *Living by the Sword*, p.159, & Schiff *et al.*, p.25. According to Green, the US Embassy in Beirut subsequently summarised casualty figures from Israeli air strikes on Beirut alone from the period 1 April until 17 July as being 438 killed and 2,479 injured.

9 E.R. interview, July 2005 & July 2012.

10 Brigadier General Ori Manos, 'The War of Artillery Commander of Northern Command', IDF Artillery Heritage website, beithatotahn.org.il; O'Ballance, *Civil War in Lebanon*; Frenkel *et al.*, 'Ground Raid'; 'Operation Harpoon', https://archive.li/3bu6H; *IAF Magazine*, Vol. 135 (1 October 2000); *Davar*, different issues from 1979, 1980 and 1981 (all in Hebrew), *Ma'ariv*, different issues from 1980; Yosef Nisimov, '41 Years Ago: Operation deep inside Lebanon that Benni Gantz took part in' (TV-documentary in Hebrew), *Channel 20* (2021).

11 Green, *Living by the Sword*, p.164.

12 'Jabbar', interview, 03/2006; & 'Hussam', interviews, 10/2016 and 04/2018.

ABOUT THE AUTHORS

TOM COOPER

Tom Cooper is an Austrian aerial warfare analyst and historian. Following a career in the worldwide transportation business – during which he established a network of contacts in the Middle East and Africa – he moved into narrow-focus analysis and writing on small, little-known air forces and conflicts, about which he has collected extensive archives. This has resulted in specialisation in Middle Eastern, African and Asian air forces. As well as authoring and co-authoring 560 books and over 1,000 articles, he has co-authored the *Arab MiGs* book series – a six-volume, in-depth analysis of the Arab air forces at war with Israel, in the 1955–73 period. Cooper has been working as editor of the five @War series since 2017.

EFIM SANDLER

Born in the Union of Soviet Socialist Republics, Efim Sandler is a veteran of the Israeli Defence Force Armoured Corps and is currently living in the USA. An enthusiastic historian since his youth, he developed a deep interest in the armoured warfare of the Arab–Israeli Wars and conflicts in the former USSR, and has been collecting related information for decades. After helping in the preparation of numerous related articles, and articles about the IDF's presence in Lebanon from 1982–2000, this is his first book.